CHRISTMAS

CHRISTMAS

hamlyn

First published in Great Britain in 1998
by Hamlyn, a division of Octopus Publishing Group Ltd
2–4 Heron Quays, London E14 4JP

This edition published 2004 by Octopus Publishing Group Ltd

ISBN 0 600 61229 5

Printed in China

NOTES

Both metric and imperial measurements have been given in all
recipes. Use one set of measurements only and not a
mixture of both.

Standard level spoon measurements are used in all recipes.
1 tablespoon = one 15 ml spoon
1 teaspoon = one 5 ml spoon

Eggs should be medium to large unless otherwise stated.
The Department of Health advises that eggs should not be
consumed raw. This book contains dishes made with raw or
lightly cooked eggs. It is prudent for more vulnerable people
such as pregnant and nursing mothers, invalids, the elderly,
babies and young children to avoid uncooked or lightly cooked
dishes made with eggs. Once prepared, these dishes should
be kept refrigerated and used promptly.

Milk should be full fat unless otherwise stated.

Meat and poultry should be cooked thoroughly. To test if poultry
is cooked, pierce the flesh through the thickest part with a
skewer or fork – the juices should run clear, never pink or red.

Do not re-freeze a dish that has been frozen previously.

Pepper should be freshly ground black pepper unless
otherwise stated.

Fresh herbs should be used, unless otherwise stated. If
unavailable, use dried herbs as an alternative but halve the
quantities stated.

Measurements for canned food have been given as a standard
metric equivalent.

Nuts and nut derivatives
This book includes dishes made with nuts and nut derivatives.
It is advisable for customers with known allergic reactions to
nuts and nut derivatives and those who may be potentially
vulnerable to these allergies, such as pregnant and nursing
mothers, invalids, the elderly, babies and children, to avoid
dishes made with nuts and nut oils. It is also prudent to check
the labels of pre-prepared ingredients for the possible inclusion
of nut derivatives.

Ovens should be preheated to the specified temperature – if
using a fan-assisted oven, follow the manufacturer's
instructions for adjusting the time and the temperature.

Contents

Introduction

Christmas is traditionally a time when people like to eat, drink and make merry with their friends and family. Sharing fine food with those closest to you can be one of the great joys of Christmas

Christmas can also be hard work. It can be daunting too, especially if this is the first time you have taken on the role of catering for a large group over the Christmas festivities.

The best way of dealing with this is to think well ahead and not to be caught unawares and unprepared.

THINKING AHEAD

At its best, Christmas cooking begins a long time before the day itself. The more you can do in advance, the easier you will find it to cope with all the preparations that simply cannot be done in advance of the day.

The early advance preparations for Christmas – in particular, making the pudding and the cake – can make the day itself even more enjoyable.

Mincemeat, Christmas pudding and Christmas cake will all improve with a long maturing time. Three months is the normal period of time these traditional Christmas fare dishes are given to develop; it can be a shorter period of time than that but any longer may affect the freshness of the dish. Any recipes made

in advance should be tightly sealed to keep them fresh and moist. Do remember though, that puddings, mincemeat and cakes can also be made very successfully even at the last possible moment.

A freezer is a great asset when it comes to taking the stress out of Christmas catering, making it a lot easier and more relaxed. Pastry cases, pies, mince pies, stuffings, soups and other useful fill-ins for odd meals that can crop up between traditional meals can all be made in advance and then frozen.

Cake decorations should be made at least a week in advance and can easily be made 3–8 weeks ahead. When using dark coloured marzipan you will need to give yourself some time, because if you put it on white icing before either is quite dry the colour may seep on to the icing.

CHRISTMAS DAY

For most people, the pièce de résistance on Christmas Day is the turkey. It's obviously best, for maximum flavour, to buy a fresh bird. It's a good idea to take it out of the refrigerator some time on Christmas Eve, to allow it to come to room temperature so that it heats up as soon as you put it in the oven when the time comes to cook it.

Fresh turkey will give the best flavour but frozen turkey can be used instead. Allow plenty of time for the bird to defrost slowly and completely before you come to cook it. Put it in the refrigerator anything from 2 to 6 days in advance of Christmas Eve, and leave it to defrost gradually (see chart opposite). Then, as with a fresh bird, take it out of the refrigerator at the last possible moment on Christmas Eve, to allow it to come to room temperature.

Once you have removed the turkey from the refrigerator, now is a good time to put in anything that needs chilling before the celebrations start. That includes the wine, champagne, mineral water and any drinks for the children.

If you want the turkey to taste really special, make a really good, out-of-the-ordinary stuffing (see pages 35 and 36) and then serve the turkey with all the trimmings, (see pages 34, 38 and 39).

COUNTDOWN TO CHRISTMAS

• 3–6 months in advance – make the Christmas Puddings (see page 12).

• 3 months in advance – make the Rich Christmas Cake (see page 13). The cake should be stored in an airtight container and drizzled occasionally with a little brandy or sherry.

• 2 months in advance – make the Rum Butter (see page 44) and Brandy Butter (see page 45), and freeze.

• 6 weeks in advance – make the Mincemeat (see page 16). Store in sealed, sterilised jars in a cool place.

• 4–6 weeks in advance – order your fresh turkey.

• at least 2 weeks in advance – make the pastry for the mince pies. As soon as both mincemeat and pastry are made, make Rich Mince Pies (see page 17) and put them in the freezer.

• 1 week in advance – do the bulk of the shopping, leaving fresh fruit and vegetables until nearer the day, preferably until Christmas Eve so that they will be really fresh on Christmas Day itself.

• 2–7 days in advance, according to weight, remove the frozen turkey from the freezer and thaw in the refrigerator (see chart below for thawing times). It should be thoroughly defrosted by the time you go to bed on Christmas Eve. To test if the bird is completely defrosted, insert a metal skewer into the breast. If the skewer is freezing to the touch on withdrawal from the bird, the turkey is not completely defrosted.

• 2–3 days in advance – make Christmas Shortbread (see page 20).

• 2 days in advance, make any last-minute Christmas Puddings (see page 43).

• Christmas Eve – shop for your fresh fruit and vegetables. Make the stock for the gravy (see page 32) using the turkey giblets. Prepare the vegetables and make the stuffing. Take enough mince pies out of the freezer for Christmas Day. Before you go to bed, take the fresh turkey or the defrosted frozen turkey out of the refrigerator and put it in a cool place. Take the Brandy Butter and Rum Butter out of the freezer and put in the refrigerator. Finally, fill the space left in the refrigerator with all the drinks which need to be chilled.

TURKEY THAWING AND COOKING GUIDE				
WEIGHT	NUMBER OF SERVINGS	THAWING TIME IN A COOL ROOM (BELOW 15°C/60°F)	COOKING TIME AT 190°C (375°F), GAS 5 WITHOUT FOIL	COOKING TIME AT 190°C (375°F), GAS 5 WITH FOIL
1.4–2.25 kg/3–5 lb	4–6	20 hrs	1½–1¾ hrs	1¾–2 hrs
2.75–3.25 kg/6–7 lb	7–9	30 hrs	1¾–2 hrs	2–2¼ hrs
3.5–4 kg/8–9 lb	10–14	36 hrs	2–2½ hrs	2½–2¾ hrs
4.5–5 kg/10–11 lb	15–16	45 hrs	2¼–2¾ hrs	2½–3 hrs
5.5–6 kg/12–13 lb	17–18	48 hrs	2¾–3 hrs	3–3¼ hrs
6.5–8 kg/14–17 lb	19–25	48 hrs	3¼–3½ hrs	3½–3¾ hrs
8.5–12 kg/18–22 lb	26–37	48 hrs	3½–3¾ hr	3¾–4 hrs
12.5 kg plus/23 lb plus	38 plus	48 hrs	3¾ hrs plus	4¼ hrs plus

CHRISTMAS WREATH CAKE
1 Working from the centre of the cake, carefully smooth the marzipan over the top and down the sides of the cake. Trim to fit.

CATERING FOR VEGETARIANS
For vegetarians, Christmas means something other than turkey. Vegetarians often complain that they cannot face the prospect of yet another nut roast for Christmas, and it is with this in mind that there are some less ubiquitous suggestions, such as Tomato and Raspberry Soup (see page 48), followed by Feta and Roasted Vegetable Pie (see page 51), accompanied by Courgettes with Orange (see page 49) and Potato and Leek Bake (see page 46). Add a Christmas Pudding (see page 43) and you have a meatless festive feast.

PARTY CATERING
Entertaining large numbers is part of Christmas, but it is important to bear in mind that during this season of indulgence lighter snacks may not only be the easiest option for the host but also the preferred choice of the guest. Simple suggestions for light refreshments for

2 Lift the ready-to-roll icing carefully over the cake, supporting it with a rolling pin. Smooth the icing over the top then the sides of the cake so that the excess icing is at the base.

larger parties include Crispy Ricotta Parcels (see page 74), Chicken Liver and Bacon Kebabs (see page 78) and Smoked Salmon Blinis (see page 81). The three dips, Houmous, Taramasalata, and Guacamole (see pages 82–83), are all quick and easy to prepare, perfect when catering for big groups.

Delicious drinks combining flavour with a seasonal touch, ideal for entertaining larger groups, include Claret Cup (see page 86), Spiced Mulled Wine (see page 88) and Mulled Ale (see page 89), as well as the more exotic Champagne Strawberry Cup (see page 91) and, for those who prefer non-alcoholic refreshment, Fruit Punch and Grape Punch (see pages 93 and 94).

ROYAL ICING
This is a traditional icing used to cover celebration cakes. Depending on the consistency, it may be used for flat icing, peaked icing or for piping on to cakes.

3 Lightly knead the fern green and citrus green coloured portions of marzipan together to give a marbled effect. Roll out thinly and cut into 8 ivy leaves using a cutter.

- 2 egg whites
- ¼ teaspoon lemon juice
- 500 g/1 lb icing sugar, sieved
- 1 teaspoon glycerine

1 Place the egg whites and the lemon juice in a clean bowl. Using a clean wooden spoon, stir the contents to break up the egg whites.
2 Add sufficient icing sugar to form the consistency of single cream. Continue mixing whilst adding small quantities of icing sugar until it is all used up, then stir in the glycerine until well blended.
3 Allow the royal icing to settle before using: cover the surface with a piece of damp clingfilm and seal well, excluding all the air.
4 Stir the royal icing thoroughly before use to disperse any air bubbles, then adjust the consistency if necessary. Use as required.

Makes 500 g/1 lb

4 Roll out the holly green marzipan and, using a holly leaf cutter, cut out 4 leaves. Mark the leaves with veins and twist them to give a realistic shape. Leave to dry overnight.

5 Wrap a rolling pin with non-stick baking paper. Drizzle the melted chocolate quickly backwards and forwards, across the rolling pin. Allow the chocolate to set.

6 Carefully arrange the dark and light green holly leaves and the ivy leaves in a wreath shape on top of the cake, attaching them with the apricot glaze.

7 Attach the red berries next to some of the holly leaves. Peel the chocolate off the baking paper, break up into twigs and insert them into the wreath. Dust lightly with icing sugar.

READY-TO-ROLL ICING

This icing is easy to make, and if you keep a jar of liquid glucose in the cupboard you can produce a quantity very quickly. Once it is made, the icing can be tinted with food colouring and used to cover all types of cakes. It is soft and pliable, suitable for moulding sugar decorations .

- 500 g/1 lb icing sugar
- 1 egg white
- 2 tablespoons liquid glucose
- icing sugar, for dusting

1 Sift the icing sugar into a bowl. Add the egg white and the glucose, mixing with a wooden spoon. Knead together until the mixture forms a ball. Place on a surface lightly dusted with icing sugar and knead until smooth and free of cracks.

2 If the icing is too soft to handle and sticky, knead in some more sieved icing sugar until it is firm and pliable. If the sugar paste dries out and becomes firm

and hard, knead in a little boiled water until the icing regains its soft texture.

3 Wrap the icing in clingfilm or store in a polythene bag with all the air excluded.

Makes 625 g/1 lb 4 oz

MARZIPAN

For a lighter colour use the egg white instead of the whole egg. Use the marzipan as soon as it is made so that it is still pliable.

- 250 g/8 oz ground almonds
- 125 g/4 oz caster sugar
- 125 g/4 oz icing sugar, sieved
- 1 teaspoon lemon juice
- a few drops of almond essence
- 1 small egg or 1 large egg white

1 Place the ground almonds, caster and icing sugars in a bowl. Stir until evenly mixed. Make a 'well' in the centre and add the lemon juice, almond essence and enough beaten egg or egg white to mix to

a soft but firm dough.

2 Lightly dust a surface with sieved icing sugar and knead the marzipan until it is smooth and free from cracks.

3 Store wrapped in clingfilm. Tint with food colouring if required, and use for moulding decorations or covering cakes.

Makes 500 g/1 lb marzipan

Christmas Fare

Mincemeat and Clementine Pie

icing sugar, for dusting

PASTRY:

75 g/3 oz plain flour

75 g/3 oz wholemeal flour

75 g/3 oz chilled butter, diced

50 g/2 oz ground almonds

25 g/1 oz caster sugar

grated rind of 1 orange

1 egg, beaten

FILLING:

375 g/12 oz mincemeat (see page 16)

3 clementines, peeled and segmented

1 To make the pastry, place the plain and wholemeal flours in a bowl, add the diced butter and rub in with the fingertips until the mixture resembles fine breadcrumbs. Stir in the ground almonds, sugar and orange rind, then add the egg and mix to a firm dough.

2 Knead the dough briefly on a lightly floured surface, then roll out and line a 20 cm/ 8 inch flan tin. Gather up the pastry trimmings, reroll and cut into holly shapes. Reserve 6 holly shapes and attach the remainder to the edge of the pastry case with a little water. Chill the pastry shell for 30 minutes, if time permits.

3 Mix the mincemeat and clementine segments in a bowl, then spread the mixture over the pastry case. Arrange the reserved holly shapes over the top. Bake in a preheated oven, 200°C (400°F), Gas Mark 6, for 25–30 minutes until the pastry is golden brown. Dust with icing sugar and serve warm or cold.

Serves 6

Preparation time: 20 minutes

Cooking time: 25–30 minutes

Oven temperature: 200°C (400°F), Gas Mark 6

Traditional Christmas Puddings

In the past, Christmas puddings were made during the last weekend of November – everyone in the family taking a turn at stirring on 'Stir-up Sunday' and the puddings were eaten the following year. Nowadays it is more usual to make the puddings 3–6 months in advance – although you can make them at the last minute if you have to.

- 125 g/4 oz self-raising flour
- 175 g/6 oz fresh white breadcrumbs
- 175 g/6 oz currants
- 175 g/6 oz sultanas
- 125 g/4 oz stoned dates
- 250 g/8 oz stoned raisins
- 175 g/6 oz shredded suet
- 50 g/2 oz cut mixed peel
- 50 g/2 oz blanched almonds, chopped
- 1 small apple, peeled, cored and grated
- grated rind and juice of 1 small orange
- ½ teaspoon mixed spice
- ¼ teaspoon ground or grated nutmeg
- ½ teaspoon salt
- 3 eggs
- 4 tablespoons brown ale or cider
- 250 g/8 oz soft dark brown sugar
- lard, for greasing basins
- 3-4 tablespoons brandy, to serve

1 Place all the ingredients in a large bowl, stirring well to mix.

2 Grease 1 x 1.2 litre/2 pint pudding basin and 1 x 600 ml/1 pint pudding basin well with lard. Fill each basin just over three-quarters full and bury one silver coin, wrapped in foil, in each. Cover with greased greaseproof paper and foil or a pudding cloth. Tie securely with string.

3 Place each pudding in a saucepan and pour in boiling water to come halfway up the sides. Boil for 6–8 hours depending on size, topping up with more boiling water as necessary. Remove the puddings from the pans and leave overnight to cool completely.

4 Remove the coverings and cover again with fresh greased greaseproof paper and foil or a pudding cloth. Store the puddings in a cool, dry place.

5 To serve, reboil the puddings for 3–4 hours, depending on size, then turn out on to a warm dish and serve with Rum Butter or Brandy Butter (see pages 44–45). To ignite the pudding, warm the brandy, pour all over the pudding and set alight carefully.

Makes 1 large and 1 small pudding
Preparation time: about 30 minutes, plus cooling
Cooking time: 6–8 hours, plus 3–4 hours before serving

Rich Christmas Cake

This deliciously rich fruit cake is usually served undecorated. To ice the cake, brush with apricot glaze (see page 14) and then cover with 1 kg/2 lb marzipan (see page 9) and 2–3 coats of thin royal icing (see page 8). Alternatively, if short of time, use purchased white marzipan and 2 kg/2 lb white ready-to-roll icing.

- 125 g/4 oz self-raising flour
- 200 g/7 oz plain flour
- ¼ teaspoon salt
- 1 teaspoon ground mixed spice
- ½ teaspoon ground cinnamon
- ½ teaspoon ground nutmeg
- 250 g/8 oz butter or margarine
- 250 g/8 oz soft dark brown or dark muscovado sugar
- 2 teaspoons black treacle
- 5 eggs
- 50 ml/2 fl oz medium dry sherry or strained cold tea
- 1½ teaspoons vanilla essence
- 250g/8 oz currants
- 250 g/8 oz sultanas
- 250 g/8 oz stoned raisins
- 250 g/8 oz seedless raisins
- 75 g/3 oz cut mixed peel
- 50 g/2 oz ground almonds
- 75 g/3 oz glacé cherries
- finely grated rind of 1 lemon
- 3–4 tablespoons brandy

1 Grease and line a 23 cm/9 inch round or 20 cm/8 inch square cake tin, using a double thickness of greased greaseproof paper. Line the outside with several thicknesses of brown paper, standing at least 5 cm/2 inches above the top of the tin.
2 Sift the flours into a bowl with the salt, mixed spice, cinnamon and nutmeg.
3 In a large bowl, cream the butter or margarine with the sugar until light. Beat in the treacle.
4 Lightly beat together the eggs, sherry or tea, and vanilla essence.
5 Gradually beat half of the egg mixture into the creamed mixture. Fold in a third of the mixed flours. Continue to add the egg and flour mixtures alternately. Mix in all the remaining ingredients except the brandy. Turn into the prepared tin and smooth the top.

6 Bake in a preheated oven, 140°C (275°F), Gas Mark 1, for about 4–4½ hours until a skewer inserted into the centre of the cake comes out clean. Cover the cake with a double layer of greaseproof paper if it starts to brown too much during cooking.
7 Leave to cool in the tin, then turn out on to a wire rack to cool completely. Prick all over with a fine skewer and and spoon brandy on top.
8 Store the cake in an airtight tin and leave to mature for about 3 months.

Makes 1 x 23 cm/9 inch round or 1 x 20 cm/8 inch square cake
Preparation time: 45 minutes
Cooking time: 4–4½ hours
Oven temperature: 140°C (275°F), Gas Mark 1

Christmas Wreath Cake

A simple but stunning cake iced with pristine white icing and topped with a wreath of marzipan holly and ivy and chocolate twigs. See page 8 for step-by-step instructions.

- 1 x 20 cm/8 inch square Rich Christmas Cake (see page 13)
- 4 tablespoons apricot glaze (see right)
- 1 kg/2 lb white marzipan
- 25 cm/10 inch square thick cakeboard
- 1 kg/2 lb white ready-to-roll icing
- 75 g/3 oz dark chocolate, broken into pieces
- holly red, light holly green, dark holly green, citrus green and fern green food colourings
- a little icing sugar, for sifting

1 Brush the cake with 3 tablespoons of the apricot glaze and cover with marzipan (see page 9), reserving 175 g/6 oz for the decoration. Place the cake on the cakeboard. Dampen the marzipan and cover with the ready-to-roll icing (see page 9). Use any icing trimmings to make red berries, colouring the icing with holly red food colouring. Dry on non-stick baking paper.
2 Melt the chocolate in a heatproof bowl over a pan of hot water. Wrap a rolling pin with non-stick baking paper, securing with tape. Set the pin on a baking sheet lined with non-stick baking paper, then drizzle the chocolate quickly backwards and forwards, across the width of the rolling pin. Allow the chocolate to set.
3 Divide the marzipan into four. Colour one quarter light holly green, one quarter dark holly green, one quarter citrus green and one quarter fern green. Place the light and dark holly green marzipan in individual plastic bags to prevent it from drying out.
4 Lightly knead the remaining two shades of marzipan together to give a marbled effect. Roll out thinly on a surface lightly dusted with icing sugar and cut into eight ivy leaves using a cutter. Mark them with veins using a knife and twist slightly to give a realistic shape. Leave to dry overnight on non-stick baking paper.
5 Roll out the light holly green marzipan and, using a holly leaf cutter, cut out four leaves. Mark the leaves with veins and twist to give a realistic shape. Repeat with the dark holly green marzipan. Leave to dry overnight on non-stick baking paper.
6 Arrange the leaves in a wreath shape on top of the cake, attaching them with apricot glaze. Attach the red berries next to some of the holly leaves.
7 Carefully peel the chocolate off the baking paper, break up into twigs and insert them into the wreath. Dust lightly with sieved icing sugar to look like snow. Tie a ribbon around the cake if you wish.

Makes 1 x 20 cm/8 inch square cake
Preparation time: about 1 hour, plus drying

Apricot Glaze

It is always a good idea to make a large quantity of apricot glaze, especially when making celebration cakes.

- 500 g/1 lb apricot jam
- 3 tablespoons water

1 Place the apricot jam and water in a saucepan and heat gently, stirring occasionally until the jam has melted.
2 Boil the jam rapidly for 1 minute, then strain through a sieve. Rub through as much of the fruit as possible, using a wooden spoon. Discard the contents of the sieve.
3 Pour the apricot glaze into a clean, sterilized jar, seal with a clean lid and cool. Refrigerate for up to 2 months.

Makes 500 g/1 lb
Preparation time: 5 minutes
Cooking time: 6 minutes

Mincemeat

- 500 g/1 lb currants, chopped
- 500 g/1 lb sultanas, chopped
- 500 g/1 lb seedless raisins, chopped
- 500 g/1 lb cut mixed peel
- 125 g/4 oz blanched almonds, finely chopped
- 500 g/1 lb cooking apples, peeled, cored and coarsely grated
- 500 g/1 lb soft dark brown sugar
- 250 g/8 oz shredded suet, chopped
- 1 teaspoon ground or grated nutmeg
- 1 teaspoon ground cinnamon
- 1 teaspoon mixed spice
- grated rind of 2 lemons
- juice of 1 lemon
- 2–4 tablespoons brandy

1 Put the currants, sultanas, raisins, mixed peel and almonds into a large bowl. Add the apples, sugar, suet, spices and lemon rind and juice and stir to mix thoroughly.

2 Cover the bowl with clingfilm and leave to stand for 2 days.

3 Remove the clingfilm and stir the mincemeat again very thoroughly, pouring off any excess liquid. Stir in the brandy. Pack the mincemeat into clean sterilized jars and seal well. Label and store in a cool dry place for about 6 weeks before use.

Makes about 3.5 kg/7 lb
Preparation time: 20–30 minutes, plus standing

Rich Mince Pies

- 250 g/8 oz mincemeat (see page 16)

PASTRY:
- 250 g/8 oz plain flour
- 75 g/3 oz chilled butter, diced
- 50 g/2 oz ground almonds
- 25 g/1 oz caster sugar
- grated rind of 1 orange
- 1 egg, beaten
- 2–3 tablespoons orange juice

TO DECORATE:
- egg white, to glaze
- caster sugar, for sprinkling

1 To make the pastry, place the flour in a bowl, add the diced butter and rub in with the fingertips until the mixture resembles fine breadcrumbs. Stir in the ground almonds, sugar and orange rind, then add the egg and orange juice and mix to a firm dough.

2 Knead the dough briefly on a lightly floured surface, then roll out thinly and stamp out 12 x 7.5 cm/3 inch rounds with a pastry cutter. Line 12 bun tins with the pastry, adding 1 teaspoon mincemeat to each case.

3 Roll out the remaining pastry and cut into 5 cm/2 inch rounds to cover the mince pies. Dampen the edges and press down lightly to seal. Brush the tops of the mince pies with egg white and sprinkle lightly with the sugar.

4 Bake in a preheated oven, 200°C (400°F), Gas Mark 6, for 20 minutes until golden. Leave to cool slightly in the tins, then transfer to a wire rack.

Makes 12
Preparation time: 20 minutes, plus cooling
Cooking time: 20 minutes
Oven temperature: 200°C (400°F), Gas Mark 6

Stollen

This German 'cakebread', traditionally served at Christmas, is quite delicious. It is a slow riser because of the large amount of fruit but well worth the time it takes to make.

- 25 g/1 oz fresh yeast or 15 g/½ oz fast-action dried yeast
- 2 tablespoons warm water
- 75 g/3 oz caster sugar
- pinch of salt
- 6 tablespoons warm milk
- 2 tablespoons rum
- few drops of almond essence
- 425 g/14 oz plain flour
- 1 egg, beaten
- 150 g/5 oz unsalted butter, softened
- 50 g/2 oz raisins
- 50 g/2 oz glacé cherries, chopped, washed and dried
- 50 g/2 oz currants
- 25 g/1 oz angelica, chopped
- 50 g/2 oz cut mixed peel
- 40 g/1½ oz flaked almonds
- sifted icing sugar, to serve

1 Blend the yeast in the warm water. Dissolve 50 g/2 oz of the sugar and the salt in the milk. Add the rum, almond essence and yeast liquid.
2 Sift the flour into a bowl, making a well in the centre. Add the yeast mixture, egg, 75 g/3 oz of the softened butter cut into small pieces, and the fruit and nuts. Mix to a soft dough and knead for 10 minutes by hand, or 4–5 minutes in a large electric mixer fitted with a dough hook.

3 Return the dough to the bowl, cover with a damp cloth and leave to rise in a warm place until doubled in size – about 2 hours.
4 Knock back the dough and knead it until smooth, then roll it out on a lightly floured surface to a rectangle about 30 x 20 cm/12 x 8 inches.
5 Melt the remaining butter and brush liberally over the dough, then sprinkle with the remaining caster sugar. Fold one long side over just beyond the centre, and then fold over the other long side to overlap the first piece well. Press lightly together and slightly taper the ends.
6 Place the loaf on a greased baking sheet, brush with melted butter and leave in a warm place until almost doubled in size.
7 Bake in a preheated oven, 190°C (375°F), Gas Mark 5, for about 45 minutes until well risen and browned. Cool on a wire rack. To serve, dredge heavily with sifted icing sugar and cut into fairly thin slices.

Makes 1
Preparation time: 30 minutes, plus rising and cooling
Cooking time: about 45 minutes
Oven temperature: 190°C (375°F), Gas Mark 5

Christmas Shortbread

- 125 g/4 oz unsalted butter
- 50 g/2 oz caster sugar
- 150 g/5 oz plain flour
- 25 g/1 oz rice flour
- caster sugar, to serve

1 Place the butter and sugar in a bowl and cream together until fluffy. Sift in the flours and work to form a soft dough. Knead lightly until smooth.

2 Roll the dough into a log shape, wrap in clingfilm and chill for 30 minutes.

3 Cut the roll into slices and place on a greased baking sheet. Bake in a preheated oven, 180°C (350°F), Gas Mark 4, for 15–20 minutes until golden round the edges. Dredge with caster sugar and cool on a wire rack.

Makes about 12
Preparation time: 10 minutes
Cooking time: 15–20 minutes
Oven temperature: 180°C (350°F), Gas Mark 4

Chocolate Yule Log

- 3 eggs
- 75 g/3 oz caster sugar
- 75 g/3 oz plain flour, sifted twice
- 1 tablespoon hot water
- 1 teaspoon vanilla essence
- 30 cm/12 inch rectangular silver cakeboard
- icing sugar, for dusting

FILLING AND TOPPING:

- 175 g/6 oz sugar
- 125 ml/4 fl oz water
- 6 egg yolks
- 375 g/12 oz unsalted butter, softened
- 250 g/8 oz plain chocolate, melted and cooled

1 Place the eggs and caster sugar in a large bowl and whisk together until very thick and fluffy. Fold in the flour, water and vanilla essence gently but thoroughly. Pour the mixture into a 38 x 26 cm/15 x 10½ inch Swiss roll tin, and bake in a preheated oven, 220°C (425°F), Gas Mark 7, for 8–10 minutes until golden.

2 Turn out the cake on to a sheet of sugared greaseproof paper set on a damp tea towel. Trim the crusty edges, then roll up with the paper inside and leave to cool.

3 To make the filling and topping, place the sugar and water in a small saucepan and stir over a low heat until the sugar is dissolved. Bring to the boil, then boil without stirring until the temperature reaches 110°C (230°F) on a sugar thermometer.

4 Whisk the eggs yolks in a large bowl and continue to whisk while pouring on the syrup in a thin stream. Whisk until thick and cool. Gradually whisk in the butter and finally fold in the melted chocolate.

5 Unroll the cake and spread with half of the chocolate butter cream. Roll up neatly and place on a silver cakeboard. Cut off the end of the roll at an angle and attach to one side of the roll to resemble a branch.

6 Cover the cake evenly with the remaining chocolate butter cream and score the surface with the tines of a fork to resemble bark. Chill in the refrigerator until firm. To serve, dust the cake with icing sugar.

Makes 1

Preparation time: 1 hour, plus cooling and chilling

Cooking time: 8–10 minutes.

Oven temperature: 220°C (425°F), Gas Mark 7

Christmas
Eve

Cream of Chicken Soup

500 g/1 lb chicken pieces, skinned

1 onion, chopped

1 garlic clove, chopped

1 leek, sliced

2 carrots, sliced thinly

1 celery stick, sliced

600 ml/1 pint water

600 ml/1 pint chicken stock

150 ml/¼ pint single cream

salt and pepper

TO GARNISH:

chopped fresh parsley

paprika

1 Place the chicken pieces in a large saucepan. Add the onion, garlic and remaining vegetables. Season to taste. Add the water and slowly bring to the boil, skimming off any scum that rises to the surface.

2 Cover and simmer over a low heat for 30 minutes. Stir in the stock and bring to the boil. Lower the heat, cover and simmer for a further 30 minutes. Adjust the seasoning.

3 Lift out the chicken pieces with a slotted spoon. Remove and discard the bones. Place the meat in a blender or food processor. Add the soup and blend until smooth (this may be done in two batches).

4 Return the soup to the pan. If it is too thick, thin it down with a little more stock or water. Stir in the cream and heat through, but do not let the soup boil. Serve sprinkled with chopped parsley and paprika.

Serves 6

Preparation time: about 15 minutes

Cooking time: about 1½ hours

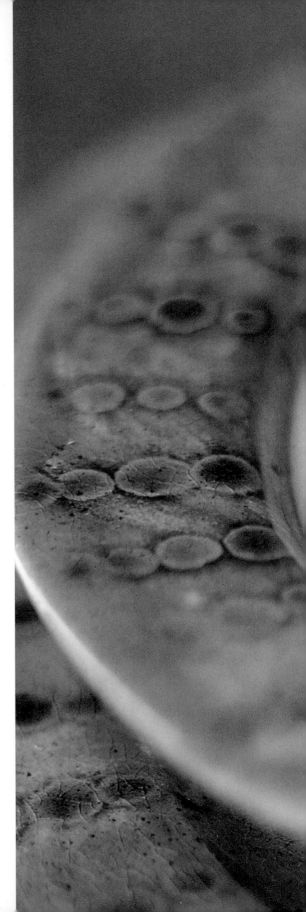

Winter Salad

- 2 green-skinned dessert apples
- 2 red-skinned dessert apples
- 2 conference pears
- 2 tablespoons lemon juice
- 1 head of celery, trimmed and sliced
- 50–75 g/2–3 oz shelled walnuts
- 4 spring onions, trimmed and sliced finely
- 4 tablespoons French dressing
- 2 tablespoons single cream

1 Core the apples and slice thinly. Place in a large bowl. Peel, core and slice the pears and add to the bowl with the lemon juice. Stir lightly but thoroughly to mix, to prevent the fruit discolouring, then pour off the excess lemon juice.

2 Add the sliced celery, walnuts and sliced spring onions. Mix together the French dressing and cream and, whisking with a fork, pour the dressing over the salad. Toss lightly but thoroughly, then turn into a salad bowl, cover closely, and chill in the refrigerator until required.

Serves 8
Preparation time: about 20 minutes

Cold Baked Ham

The soaking time for the gammon depends on how salty it is, so check with your supplier when you buy the joint. Soak overnight if in doubt.

- **2.5–4 kg/5–8 lb gammon joint, either on the bone or boned and rolled**
- **2 bay leaves**
- **2 tablespoons demerara sugar**
- **150 ml/¼ pint ginger ale**

GLAZE:
- **3 tablespoons ginger marmalade**
- **6 tablespoons demerara sugar**

1 Place the gammon in a large saucepan of cold water and leave to soak for 2–12 hours.

2 Drain the gammon, then weigh and calculate the cooking time at 25 minutes per 500 g/1 lb, plus 20 minutes. For a joint over 3 kg/6 lb allow 20 minutes per 500 g/1 lb, plus 20 minutes.

3 Return the gammon to the pan and pour in enough fresh cold water to cover. Add the bay leaves and sugar and bring to the boil. Cover, lower the heat and simmer for half the estimated cooking time.

4 Remove the gammon from the pan and strip off the skin. Stand the gammon on a large sheet of foil in a roasting tin and score the fat diagonally in a trellis pattern. Mix together the marmalade and sugar and spread over the surface of the fat.

5 Pour the ginger ale around the joint and enclose in the foil, sealing the edges firmly. Cook in a preheated oven, 190°C (375°F), Gas Mark 5,

for half the remaining cooking time.

6 Baste the gammon with the ginger ale, rewrap in the foil and cook until 20 minutes before the end of the cooking time. Fold back the foil, baste again and return to the oven. Remove from the oven and leave the gammon to cool.

Serves 10–15

Preparation time: 5 minutes, plus soaking and cooling
Cooking time: 2 hours 20 minutes–3 hours 20 minutes
Oven temperature: 190°C (375°F), Gas Mark 5

Crispy Roast Duck

- 2 kg/4 lb duckling
- 3 tarragon sprigs
- 250 g/8 oz kumquats
- 1 tablespoon orange juice
- 3 tablespoons sherry
- 1 tablespoon clear honey
- salt and pepper
- green beans, to serve

1 Dry the duckling thoroughly inside and out with kitchen paper, then season the cavity with salt and pepper. Tuck the tarragon sprigs and 4 of the kumquats inside the duckling, then place it on a rack over a roasting tin. With a needle, prick the duckling in several places to release the fat during cooking. Rub the skin with salt and roast in the centre of a preheated oven, 190°C (375°F), Gas Mark 5, for 1½ hours or until the skin is crisp and golden.

2 A few minutes before the duckling is cooked, cut the remaining kumquats lengthways in half and place in a pan with the orange juice, sherry and honey. Bring to the boil and simmer for 2 minutes, stirring constantly.

3 To serve, carve the duckling into 4 quarters, place on a warmed serving dish, spoon over the kumquats and serve with the green beans.

Serves 4
Preparation time: 15 minutes
Cooking time: about 1½ hours
Oven temperature: 190°C (375°F), Gas Mark 5

VARIATION

Duck with Orange and Brandy Sauce

1 Cook the duckling as left, but without the kumquats.

2 Meanwhile, thinly pare the rind from 2 oranges and cut into thin strips. Cover with cold water and cook for 8–10 minutes, until tender. Drain and reserve 150 ml/¼ pint of the cooking liquid.

3 Squeeze the juice from 3 oranges and 1 lemon and make up to 300 ml/½ pint with beef stock. Remove the duckling from the roasting tin and skim off the fat. Sprinkle in 1 tablespoon of flour and cook for 2 minutes, stirring.

4 Gradually stir in the reserved orange liquid, the stock mixture and 150 ml/¼ pint white wine and bring to the boil. Add 2 tablespoons of redcurrant jelly, 2 tablespoons of honey, and season. Simmer until the sauce is reduced by one-quarter.

5 Return the duckling to the roasting tin, pour over 4 tablespoons brandy and ignite. Baste with the sauce then transfer to a serving dish and sprinkle with half the orange strips. Pour the sauce into a warm sauceboat and stir in the remaining orange strips.

Mincemeat and Cranberry Tart

PASTRY:

- 250 g/8 oz self-raising flour
- 125 g/4 oz chilled butter, diced
- 75 g/3 oz caster sugar
- grated rind of 1 orange
- 1 egg, beaten

FILLING:

- 250 g/8 oz fresh or frozen cranberries, thawed
- 250 g/8 oz mincemeat (see page 16)

TO DECORATE:

- milk, to glaze
- caster sugar, for sprinkling

1 Place the flour in a bowl, add the diced butter and rub in with the fingertips until the mixture resembles fine breadcrumbs. Stir in the caster sugar and grated orange rind, then add the beaten egg and enough water to mix to a soft dough.

2 Turn out the dough on to a lightly floured surface and knead briefly. Roll out and line a 25 x 15 cm/10 x 6 inch shallow rectangular tin. Trim the edges, reserving the trimmings.

3 Stir the cranberries into the mincemeat and spread the mixture over the base of the pastry case. Reroll the reserved pastry trimmings and cut into small Christmas tree or holly shapes. Arrange the shapes over the mincemeat mixture.

4 Brush the pastry with milk and sprinkle with a little sugar. Bake in a preheated oven, 190°C (375°C), Gas Mark 5, for 25–30 minutes until the pastry is golden brown. Sprinkle with caster sugar. Cut the tart into six squares and serve warm with whipped cream or a jug of warm pouring custard, if liked.

Serves 6
Preparation time: 20 minutes
Cooking time: 25–30 minutes
Oven temperature:190°C (375°C), Gas Mark 5

Crystallized Fruits

Fruits with edible skins are suitable for crystallizing. Trim the grapes and soft fruit into small bunches or sprigs to make an attractive display. Redcurrant or strawberry leaves could also be frosted and added to the fruit.

- **selection of prepared fruit, such as grapes, redcurrants, strawberries and plums**
- **1 egg white, beaten**
- **granulated sugar, to sprinkle**

1 Dip the fruit into the egg white, or brush lightly with the egg white, and place on a wire rack set over a plate, or in a colander over a large bowl.

2 Sprinkle the fruit generously with the sugar, covering as much of the surfaces as possible, and leave to stand until the sugar has hardened.

Serves 6
Preparation time: 10 minutes, plus standing

Christmas

Day

Vegetable Soup with Pesto

3 tablespoons olive oil

2 onions, chopped

6 small leeks, trimmed and diced

4 carrots, trimmed and diced

6 garlic cloves, sliced

8 large handfuls salad leaves, such as watercress, young spinach leaves,
mustard greens, parsley or sorrel, very finely chopped

1.5 litres/2½ pints vegetable stock or water

5 tablespoons ready-made pesto

salt and pepper

TO GARNISH:

watercress or parsley sprigs

cheese straws (optional)

1 Heat the olive oil in a large saucepan. Add the onions, leeks, carrots and garlic and cook over a gentle heat, stirring occasionally, for 5 minutes until softened.

2 Stir in the salad leaves and cook, stirring, until they have wilted. Pour in the stock, bring to the boil, then simmer gently for about 25 minutes.

3 Season to taste with salt and pepper, then stir in the pesto and heat through.

4 Serve in warmed bowls, garnished with watercress or parsley sprigs, and with a cheese straw on the side, if liked.

Serves 10

Preparation time: 20 minutes

Cooking time: 25–30 minutes

Roast Turkey

The recipe below serves 8 but do choose a turkey whose weight is appropriate for the number of people you wish to feed. Weigh your turkey after it has been stuffed to work out the cooking time (see page 7).

- 5–6 kg /10–12 lb oven-ready turkey, with giblets
- 1 small onion, peeled and halved
- Pecan Stuffing (see page 35) or Cranberry and Orange Stuffing (see page 36)
- 40 g/1½ oz butter or margarine, softened
- 2 tablespoons vegetable oil
- salt and pepper

1 Make the giblet stock (see right). Wash the inside of the turkey and dry thoroughly with kitchen paper. Pack the chosen stuffing loosely into the neck of the bird. Do not stuff the body cavity because this may prevent the bird from cooking through completely. Place the onion in the body cavity, season to taste and lightly truss the bird.
2 Trussing keeps the stuffing in position and also holds the turkey together so that it will cook evenly and sit easily for carving. To truss the turkey, set it breast up and pull back the legs. Push a threaded trussing needle through the bird at the joint of the knee. Turn the bird on to its breast, pull the neck skin over the neck cavity and secure with a stitch which passes through both the wings. Next, turn the bird on to its side, pull the ends of the string from both the leg and wing together and fasten them firmly. Finally, turn the bird breast side up, tuck the tail into the body cavity and tie the drumsticks together by stitching in a figure of eight under the breast bone and around the two drumsticks.
3 Once you have trussed the turkey place it in a large roasting tin and rub all over with butter. Add the oil to the tin and season the outside of the turkey with salt and pepper.
4 Roast in a preheated oven, 180°C (350°F), Gas Mark 4, for 3–3¼ hours, basting from time to time. Cover with greaseproof paper or foil when sufficiently browned. Check for doneness by inserting a skewer into the thickest part of the thigh, the juices should run clear. If they are pink, cook for a further 15 minutes and test again.
5 Transfer the turkey to a large dish. Pour off the fat from the tin and use the juices to make the Wine Gravy (see right).
6 Arrange the turkey on a warmed serving platter and serve with Wine Gravy, Bread Sauce (see page 34) and an assortment of vegetables.

Serves 8
Preparation time: about 30 minutes
Cooking time: 3–3¼ hours
Oven temperature: 180°C (350°F), Gas Mark 4

Wine Gravy

If you are going to make the Pecan Stuffing as well as the Wine Gravy, you will probably need extra giblets to make the stock. Ask your butcher for extra giblets, or use chicken livers.

- 2 tablepoons plain flour
- 150 ml/¼ pint full-bodied red wine
- few drops of gravy browning
- 2 tablespoons redcurrant jelly
- salt and pepper

GIBLET STOCK:
- giblets from a 5–6 kg/10–12 lb turkey
- 1 small onion, peeled and quartered

1 To make the giblet stock, put all the turkey giblets except the liver into a saucepan with a small onion and pour in 1.2 litres/2 pints cold water. Bring to the boil, then lower the heat, cover and simmer for 1 hour. Strain the stock and reserve.
2 Once the turkey is cooked, pour off the fat and all but 2 tablespoons of the juices from the roasting tin. Set the tin on top of the stove, add the flour and cook gently, stirring, for 1–2 minutes until golden.
3 Stir in the red wine, 450 ml/¾ pint of the giblet stock, the gravy browning and redcurrant jelly and season to taste. Cook gently for 5 minutes, stirring all the time, until the gravy is smooth and thickened, then pour into a warmed sauceboat.

Makes 600 ml/1 pint
Preparation time: about 1 hour
Cooking time: 10 minutes

Bread Sauce

A traditional sauce to serve with roast turkey, chicken or pheasant. It should have a thick, creamy consistency, with no lumps.

- 1 small onion
- 3 cloves
- 1 bay leaf
- a few sprigs of parsley
- 450 ml/¾ pint milk
- 75 g/3 oz fresh white breadcrumbs
- 40 g/1½ oz butter
- 150 ml/¼ pint single cream
- grated nutmeg, to taste
- salt and pepper
- melted butter, to serve

1 Stud the onion with the cloves and put it into a saucepan with the bay leaf, parsley and milk. Cover and bring slowly to the boil. Remove the pan from the heat and leave to infuse for 30 minutes.

2 Strain the milk into a clean saucepan, discarding the onion and herbs. Stir in the breadcrumbs and butter and cook over a very low heat for 15 minutes, stirring occasionally to prevent the sauce becoming lumpy. Stir in the cream and add nutmeg and salt and pepper to taste. Serve drizzled with a little melted butter.

Serves 8
Preparation time: 10 minutes, plus standing
Cooking time: 15 minutes

Pecan Stuffing

- heart and liver from a 6 kg/12 lb turkey
- 50 g/2 oz fresh breadcrumbs
- 50 g/2 oz shelled pecan nuts, finely chopped
- 1 egg, hardboiled and chopped
- pinch each of grated nutmeg, ground mace and dried thyme
- 1 tablespoon chopped fresh parsley
- pinch of celery salt
- 40 g/1½ oz butter
- 50 g/2 oz mushrooms, finely chopped
- 1 small onion, chopped
- 2 tablespoons dry sherry
- salt and pepper

1 Put the heart and liver into a saucepan and cover with water. Bring to the boil and simmer for 10 minutes.
2 Chop the heart and liver finely and set aside to cool.
3 Place the chopped meat in a bowl and stir in the breadcrumbs, nuts, egg, spices, parsley and celery salt.
4 Melt the butter in a saucepan, add the mushrooms and onion and cook over a moderate heat, stirring frequently, for about 5 minutes until softened. Stir into the meat mixture, add the sherry and season to taste.

**Makes enough to stuff a
6 kg/12 lb turkey**
Preparation time: 5 minutes
Cooking time: 15–20 minutes

Cranberry and Orange Stuffing

Blueberries could be used instead of cranberries, if preferred, and would also give a transatlantic flavour to this unusual stuffing. They are available in large supermarkets, fresh or frozen.

- 375 g/12 oz mixture long-grain and wild rice
- 75 g/3 oz butter
- 1 large onion, finely chopped
- 2 tablespoons chopped fresh parsley
- 1 tablespoon chopped thyme
- pinch each of ground cloves and grated nutmeg
- salt and pepper

CRANBERRY AND ORANGE SAUCE:

- 75 g/3 oz sugar
- 150 ml/¼ pint water
- grated rind and juice of 1 orange
- 250 g/8 oz fresh or frozen cranberries, thawed

1 First make the cranberry and orange sauce. Put the sugar and water into a saucepan and stir over a low heat until the sugar is dissolved. Bring to the boil and boil for 2–3 minutes. Add the orange rind and juice and the cranberries and stir with a wooden spoon, taking care not to crush the fruit. Simmer for 5 minutes until the sauce is translucent. Set aside.

2 Cook the rice in a large pan of boiling salted water for 10–12 minutes until just tender. Drain the rice into a colander, rinse under cold water and drain again.

3 Melt the butter in a saucepan and fry the onion over a moderate heat for 3–4 minutes, stirring once or twice. Remove from the heat.

4 Stir the rice, herbs, spices and the cranberry and orange sauce into the onion mixture. Season the stuffing with salt and pepper and set aside to cool completely before packing into the turkey.

Makes enough to stuff a 6 kg/12 lb turkey
Preparation time: 10 minutes, plus cooling
Cooking time: 25–30 minutes

Sesame Roast Potatoes

An exciting and elegant variation on the usual roast potato.

- 4 baking potatoes, about 175 g/6 oz each, peeled and halved lengthways
- 4 tablespoons olive oil
- 2 tablespoons sesame seeds
- salt

1 Place the potatoes cut-side down. Using a sharp knife, make cuts at 5 mm/¼ inch intervals along the length of each potato almost through to the base, so that they just hold together.

2 Heat the oil in a roasting tin in a preheated oven, 200°C (400°F), Gas Mark 6, until hot. Add the potatoes to the tin and spoon the oil evenly over each one. Roast the potatoes for 30 minutes. Baste well and sprinkle with a little salt, if liked.

3 Sprinkle the potatoes with the sesame seeds and cook for a further 30 minutes or until the potatoes are golden brown and crisp. The cuts will open out a little during cooking to make a fantail shape.

Serves 4
Preparation time: 10 minutes
Cooking time: 1–1¼ hours
Oven temperature: 200°C (400°F), Gas Mark 6

Brussels Sprouts with Chestnuts

Brussels sprouts are a traditional accompaniment to roast turkey, but many people find them a little dull. This version gives the humble sprout a new lease of life.

- 1.5 kg/3 lb Brussels sprouts, trimmed
- 2 x 220 g/7 oz cans chestnuts, drained
- vegetable stock
- 25 g/1 oz butter
- salt and pepper

1 Place the Brussels sprouts in a pan of boiling salted water. Cover and cook for 10–12 minutes until tender. Drain.

2 Put the chestnuts into a saucepan, add enough stock to cover, and heat gently until warmed through.
3 Drain the chestnuts, stir into the sprouts with the butter, and season.

Serves 10
Preparation time: 10 minutes
Cooking time: 10–12 minutes

Baby Glazed Carrots

These delicious, sweet-tasting little carrots are the perfect foil to a heavy roast dinner. Other baby vegetables could be cooked in the same way, especially baby onions and sliced courgettes.

- 25 g/1 oz butter
- 50 g/1 lb young carrots, trimmed and quartered lengthways
- pinch of sugar
- juice of ½ orange
- salt and pepper
- chopped fresh parsley, to garnish

1 Melt the butter in a saucepan, add the carrots and sugar and season. Pour in just enough water to cover and cook gently, uncovered, for 15–20 minutes until the carrots are tender and the liquid has evaporated. Add the orange juice towards the end.

2 Serve sprinkled with the parsley.

Serves 4
Preparation time: 5 minutes
Cooking time: 15–20 minutes.

Roast Parsnips

- 1 kg/2 lb parsnips, trimmed and quartered lengthways
- 4 tablespoons olive oil, for roasting
- salt and pepper
- chopped fresh parsley, to garnish (optional)

1 Place the parsnips in a pan of boiling salted water and parboil for 5 minutes, then drain.

2 Turn the parsnips into a small roasting tin and pour over the oil. Turn the parsnips so that they are well coated with the oil. Season with salt and pepper and cook in a preheated oven, 180°C (350°F), Gas Mark 4, for 45 minutes until tender, basting with the oil occasionally.

3 Serve sprinkled with parsley, if liked.

Serves 8

Preparation time: 10 minutes
Cooking time: about 45 minutes
Oven temperature: 180°C (350°F), Gas Mark 4

Bacon and Sausage Rolls

• 16 rashers of streaky bacon, rinded
• 16 pork chipolata sausages

1 Stretch the bacon rashers with the back of a knife. Wind one rasher along the length of each sausage and fasten with a wooden cocktail stick.
2 Arrange the sausage parcels on a grill rack and cook under a preheated moderate grill for about 7–8 minutes on each side.

Makes 16
Preparation time: 5 minutes
Cooking time: about 15 minutes

Christmas Puddings

These Christmas puddings do not need to mature like the traditional variety (see page 12); in fact, they can even be made about two days before Christmas. They are suitable for vegetarians.

- 250 g/8 oz dark molasses sugar
- 425 g/14 oz fresh white breadcrumbs
- 250 g/8 oz shredded vegetable suet
- ½ teaspoon salt
- 1 teaspoon mixed spice
- 375 g/12 oz sultanas
- 375 g/12 oz stoned raisins
- 250 g/8 oz currants
- 125 g/4 oz candied peel, chopped
- 50 g/2 oz blanched almonds, finely chopped
- 2 large cooking apples, peeled, cored and finely chopped
- finely grated rind and juice of ½ lemon
- 2 eggs, beaten
- 300 ml/½ pint Guinness or milk stout
- about 150 ml/¼ pint milk
- margarine, for greasing basins

1 Put the dry ingredients, sultanas, raisins, currants, candied peel and almonds into a large bowl and mix well. Add the apples with the lemon rind and juice, eggs and Guinness and stir well. Add enough milk to make a soft dropping consistency.

2 Turn the mixture into two greased 1.2 litre/2 pint pudding basins. Cover the tops of the puddings with circles of greased greaseproof paper, then with foil, or tie up the basins in a pudding cloth. Fold a pleat in the centre and tie string around the rim. Leave the puddings to stand overnight.

3 Place the basins in the top of a steamer or double boiler, or a large pan of gently bubbling water, and steam for 4–5 hours, topping up with more boiling water as necessary.

4 Remove the basins from the pan and leave to cool completely. Discard the foil and greaseproof paper and replace with fresh greaseproof paper and foil if you intend to store the puddings.

5 To serve, steam again for about 2 hours.

Makes 2 large puddings

Preparation time: about 30 minutes, plus standing and cooling
Cooking time: 4–5 hours, plus 2 hours before serving

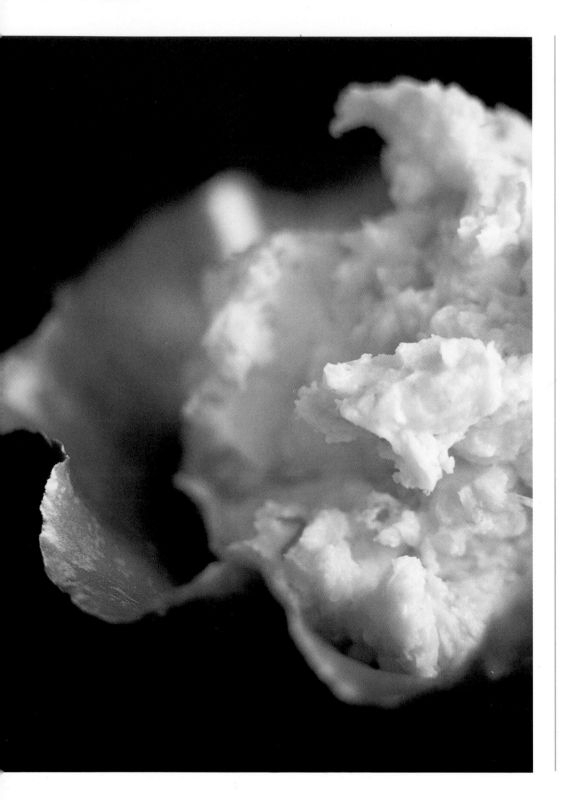

Rum Butter

A delicious variation on the better-known Brandy Butter (see right). This butter is wonderful served with any steamed pudding.

- 250 g/8 oz unsalted butter, softened
- 125 g/4 oz soft brown sugar
- 50 ml/2 fl oz light rum

1 Put the butter into a bowl and, using an electric or rotary mixer, beat until light and fluffy. Gradually beat in the brown sugar, then beat in the rum.
2 Spoon into a serving bowl and chill in the refrigerator. Serve chilled.

Makes 375 g/12 oz
Preparation time: 15 minutes, plus chilling

Brandy Butter

- 75 g/3 oz unsalted butter, softened
- 75 g/3 oz icing sugar, sifted
- finely grated rind and juice of ½ orange
- 2 tablespoons brandy

1 Put the butter in a bowl and, using an electric or rotary mixer, beat until light and fluffy. Gradually beat in the icing sugar, then beat in the orange rind and juice and the brandy.
2 Turn the brandy butter into a serving bowl and chill in the refrigerator until quite firm. Serve chilled.

Makes 175 g/6 oz
Preparation time: 10–15 minutes, plus chilling

Vegetarian
Christmas

Potato and Leek Bake

This is a variation of the famous Pommes Dauphinois – a delicious confection of potatoes and cream. The leeks add colour and flavour to the creamy dish. For the authentic French taste, add a crushed clove of garlic

1.25kg/2½ lb potatoes, peeled
500 g/1 lb leeks, trimmed and sliced
150 ml/¼ pint single cream
50 g/2 oz vegetarian Cheddar cheese, grated
25 g/1 oz fresh breadcrumbs
salt and pepper
parsley sprigs, to garnish (optional)

1 Place the potatoes in a saucepan of salted boiling water and parboil for 3 minutes. Drain and slice.
2 Place the leeks in a greased ovenproof dish and season with pepper. Arrange the potatoes on the top and pour the cream over. Cover with foil and bake in a preheated oven, 190°C (375°F), Gas Mark 5, for 45 minutes until the potatoes are tender.
3 Sprinkle with the cheese and breadcrumbs and cook under a preheated moderate grill until the top is browned. Garnish with parsley sprigs, if liked, and serve at once.

Serves 6
Preparation time: 20 minutes
Cooking time: 50 minutes
Oven temperature: 190°C (375°F), Gas Mark 5

Tomato and Raspberry Soup

- 2 tablespoons vegetable oil
- 1 onion, chopped
- 2 celery sticks, chopped
- 2 small carrots, chopped
- 2 x 425 g/14 oz cans chopped tomatoes
- 300 ml/½ pint vegetable stock
- 500 g/1 lb frozen raspberries, thawed and sieved
- 2 tablespoons lemon juice
- 2 tablespoons caster sugar (optional)
- salt and pepper

TO GARNISH:
- fresh or frozen raspberries
- 150 g/5 oz natural yogurt

1 Heat the oil in a large saucepan. Add the onion, celery and carrots and fry for 5 minutes until softened.
2 Add the tomatoes and vegetable stock and season with pepper. Bring to the boil, then simmer for 15 minutes.
3 Add the raspberry purée, lemon juice and sugar, if using. Taste for seasoning. Turn the mixture into a liquidizer or food processor and purée until smooth.
4 To serve, heat the soup through, then turn into warmed bowls and garnish each one with raspberries and a spoonful of yogurt.

Serves 6
Preparation time: 20 minutes
Cooking time: 20 minutes

Courgettes with Orange

- 750 g/1½ lb courgettes, sliced
- grated rind and juice of 2 oranges
- 25 g/1 oz butter
- pepper

1 Place the courgettes and orange rind and juice in a saucepan. Cover tightly and simmer for about 6 minutes or until the courgettes are tender.
2 Add the butter and season with pepper. Allow the butter to melt slightly, then toss until the courgettes are well coated. Serve at once.

Serves 6
Preparation time: 10 minutes
Cooking time: about 6 minutes

Cashew Nut Roll

- 40 g/1½ oz butter
- 40 g/1½ oz plain flour
- 250 ml/8 fl oz milk
- 4 small eggs, separated
- 125 g/4 oz cashew nuts, toasted lightly and ground coarsely
- pepper

FILLING:

- 500 g/1 lb tomatoes, skinned and chopped roughly
- 2 celery sticks, chopped
- 2 shallots, chopped
- ½ teaspoon dried oregano
- 2 tablespoons tomato purée
- 125 g/4 oz cashew nuts, toasted lightly and chopped coarsely

TO GARNISH:

- freshly grated vegetarian Parmesan cheese
- coriander leaves

1 Melt the butter in a small saucepan, stir in the flour and cook for 1 minute. Gradually blend in the milk, and cook until the mixture thickens. Remove the saucepan from the heat and stir in the egg yolks and ground cashew nuts. Season with pepper.

2 Whisk the egg whites stiffly and stir a spoonful of egg white into the sauce mixture. Fold in the remaining egg whites. Spread the mixture in a greased and lined 23 x 33 cm/9 x 13 inch Swiss roll tin. Bake in a preheated oven, 190°C (375°F), Gas Mark 5, for 15–20 minutes until set and golden.

3 Meanwhile, make the filling. Place the tomatoes, celery, shallots, oregano and tomato purée in a saucepan and simmer gently for 5–10 minutes until the mixture is thick and pulpy. Stir in the chopped cashew nuts, reserving a few for garnish.

4 Turn out the roll on to a hot, clean, damp tea towel, covered with a sheet of greaseproof paper. Trim the edges. Spread the filling over the roll and roll up from a short side, using the tea towel to help you roll.

5 Sprinkle with the Parmesan cheese and cashew nuts. Serve hot in slices, garnished with coriander leaves.

Serves 6

Preparation time: 15 minutes
Cooking time: 15–20 minutes
Oven temperature: 190°C (375°F), Gas Mark 5

Feta and Roasted Vegetable Pie

PASTRY:

- 125 g/4 oz self-raising flour
- 50 g/2 oz oatmeal
- 75 g/3 oz chilled butter, diced

FILLING:

- 1 aubergine, sliced
- 1 red pepper, cored, deseeded and cut into thick strips
- 1 onion, cut into wedges
- 2 courgettes, cut into sticks
- 3 tomatoes, halved
- 2 garlic cloves, chopped
- 3 tablespoons olive oil
- 2 teaspoons chopped fresh rosemary
- 125 g/4 oz feta cheese, crumbled
- 2 tablespoons freshly grated vegetarian Parmesan cheese
- salt and pepper

1 Mix the flour and oatmeal in a bowl. Add the butter and rub in with the fingertips. Add about 2 tablespoons of cold water, enough to mix to a firm dough. Turn out on to a lightly floured surface and knead briefly.

2 Roll out the pastry and use to line a 23 cm/9 inch pie plate. Fill with crumpled foil and bake in a preheated oven, 200°C (400°F), Gas Mark 6, for 15 minutes, then remove the foil and return the pastry case to the oven for 5 minutes.

3 Meanwhile, prepare the filling. Arrange the vegetables in a roasting tin. Add the garlic, oil and rosemary and season to taste. Turn the vegetables to coat them evenly with the oil. Roast at 200°C (400°F), Gas Mark 6 for 35 minutes, or until tender, turning them occasionally.

4 Remove the cooked vegetables with a slotted spoon and arrange in the pastry case. Scatter the feta cheese over the top and sprinkle with the Parmesan. Return the pie to the oven for 10 minutes until the top is crisp and golden. Serve warm or cold.

Serves 6
Preparation time: 25 minutes
Cooking time: 45 minutes
Oven temperature: 200°C (400°F), Gas Mark 6

Boxing Day

Winter Vegetable Platter with Rouille

VEGETABLE PLATTER:

selection of winter vegetables, such as
carrots, baby fennel, sea kale and
baby turnips
extra-virgin olive oil
coarse sea salt
mint leaves, to garnish

ROUILLE:

1 red pepper, cored, deseeded and chopped
2 garlic cloves, chopped
2 red chillies, cored, deseeded and chopped
6 tablespoons extra-virgin olive oil
25 g/1 oz fresh white breadcrumbs
salt and pepper

1 First prepare the rouille. Put the red pepper, garlic, chillies and olive oil into a liquidizer or food processor and process until fairly smooth. Scrape down the sides of the bowl with a spatula occasionally to make sure you blend all the ingredients evenly. Add the breadcrumbs, and salt and pepper to taste, and process again to form a thick paste. Transfer to a small bowl, cover and chill until ready to serve.

2 Prepare the vegetables according to type and size – the dish will look more attractive if all the vegetables are of a similar size, or are cut into the similar-sized pieces. Boil or steam the vegetables until just tender. Drain and refresh under cold running water, then drain again thoroughly.

3 Arrange the vegetables on a large serving platter. Drizzle with olive oil and sprinkle with sea salt. Serve with the rouille, garnished with roughly torn fresh mint leaves.

Serves 4–6

Preparation time: 30 minutes
Cooking time: 20–30 minutes

Fish Terrine

- 375 g/12 oz haddock, whiting or sole fillets, skinned
- 150 ml/¼ pint dry white wine
- 1 bouquet garni
- few strips of pared lemon rind
- 250 g/8 oz skimmed milk cheese
- 250 g/8 oz curd or full-fat soft cheese
- 2 tablespoons gelatine
- 3 egg whites
- 1 tablespoon lemon juice
- 3 tablespoons chopped fresh chives
- 250 g/8 oz cooked peeled prawns, roughly chopped
- 2 tablespoons tomato purée
- few drops of Tabasco sauce
- pepper
- a few sprigs of dill, to garnish

1 Place the fish fillets in a shallow pan with the wine, bouquet garni, lemon rind and just enough water to cover the fish. Poach, covered, over a gentle heat for 8–10 minutes until the fillets are just tender.

2 Remove the fish with a slotted spoon, drain, flake and cool. Reserve the cooking liquid.

3 Soften the two cheeses and beat together until smooth. Place 4 table-spoons of the hot fish liquid in a small bowl and sprinkle the gelatine over. Stir until the gelatine has dissolved. Leave to cool completely, then stir into the cheese mixture.

4 Whisk the egg whites until stiff and fold into the cheese mixture. Divide the mixture in halves. Into one half gently stir the cooked fish, lemon juice, chives and pepper. Pour the mixture into a wetted 1 kg/2 lb loaf tin and chill until set. Into the remaining cheese mixture stir the prawns, tomato purée and Tabasco sauce. Pour on to the fish mixture in the tin and chill until set. If you are not planning to serve the terrine immediately once it has set, cover and refrigerate.

5 To turn out the terrine, dip the loaf tin into a bowl of hot water for a few seconds, then invert on to a dish. Serve the terrine sliced, garnished with dill sprigs.

Serves 6
Preparation time: 45 minutes, plus chilling
Cooking time: 8–10 minutes

Game Pie

- 1 kg/2 lb prepared mixed game, such as venison, hare, rabbit or pheasant
- 500 g/1 lb herby sausages, skinned
- 175 g/6 oz streaky bacon, chopped
- 4 tablespoons chopped fresh parsley
- 150 ml/¼ pint chicken or game stock
- 150 ml/¼ pint dry white wine
- 2 teaspoons gelatine
- salt and pepper

MARINADE:

- 150 m/¼ pint red wine
- 2 bay leaves
- 4 juniper berries, bruised
- 1 onion, sliced
- 1 garlic clove, sliced
- few sprigs of thyme
- 2 tablespoons olive oil
- 1 teaspoon sugar

PASTRY:

- 375 g/12 oz plain flour
- ½ teaspoon salt
- 75 g/3 oz lard or white fat
- 150 ml/¼ pint milk and water mixed
- beaten egg, to glaze

1 Cut the game into strips and place in a bowl. Add the marinade ingredients and mix. Cover and refrigerate overnight. Drain the game and dry on kitchen paper. Break up the sausages with a fork and mix with the game. Add the bacon and parsley and season.

2 To make the pastry, mix the flour and salt in a bowl. Melt the lard in the milk and water mixture in a saucepan, bring to the boil, then stir into the flour and mix to form a soft dough. Wrap closely and leave to rest at room temperature for 30 minutes.

3 Roll out two-thirds of the dough on a lightly floured surface and line a 23 cm/9 in long game pie tin. Check the pastry is of even thickness and pinch together any cracks. The pastry should overlap the top of the tin.

4 Pack the filling into the tin, pressing into the corners. Roll out the remaining pastry, dampen the edges and cover the pie. Pinch the edges to seal and decorate. Make a hole in the centre of the pie and push a foil funnel into it.

5 Roll out the pastry trimmings and use to decorate the pie. Attach with the beaten egg, then glaze the whole pie. Bake in a preheated oven, 200°C (400°F), Gas Mark 6, for 1 hour, then reduce the heat to 180°C (350°F), Gas Mark 4 and bake for 1½ hours. If the crust browns too fast, cover with foil. Cool, then carefully unmould the pie. Boil the stock and white wine for 5 minutes, then sprinkle on the gelatine and stir to dissolve. Cool until it starts to set, then pour into the pie through the funnel. Chill, then serve.

Serves 8–10

Preparation time: 45 minutes, plus marinating and chilling
Cooking time: 2½ hours
Oven temperature: 200°C (400°F), Gas Mark 6, then 180°C (350°F), Gas Mark 4

Pavlova with Tropical Fruit

The egg whites should be whisked in a large dry bowl. This allows the maximum amount of air to be incorporated to produce the greatest volume. Any grease or egg yolk will prevent the whites becoming stiff. Do not put the filling into the meringue base more than 1 hour before serving, or the pavlova will go soggy.

MERINGUE:

- 4 egg whites, at room temperature
- 250 g/8 oz caster sugar
- 1 tablespoon cornflour
- 2 teaspoons vinegar
- ¼ teaspoon vanilla essence

FILLING:

- 300 ml/½ pint double cream
- 2 bananas, sliced
- 1 small pineapple, peeled and cut into cubes
- 2 passion fruit, peeled and sliced
- 2 peaches, peeled and sliced
- passion fruit seeds, to decorate

1 Whisk the egg whites with a balloon whisk in a large bowl until stiff peaks form. Add the caster sugar, one tablespoon at a time, whisking until the meringue is very stiff. Whisk in the cornflour, vinegar and vanilla essence.
2 Using a spatula, pile the meringue on to a baking sheet lined with non-stick baking paper and spread into a 23 cm/9 inch round. Hollow out the centre slightly with a spoon, then bake in a preheated oven, 150°C (300°F),

Gas Mark 2, for 1½ hours.
3 Cool, then carefully remove the paper and place the meringue on a serving dish. Whip the cream until stiff and fold in some of the fruit. Pile into the meringue and decorate with the remaining fruit. Sprinkle with the passion fruit seeds.

Serves 6–8
Preparation time: 30 minutes, plus cooling
Cooking time: 1½ hours
Oven temperature: 150°C (300°F), Gas Mark 2

New Year's Eve

Steak and Smoked Oyster Pie

1 kg/2 lb braising steak	1 tablespoon cornflour
1 large onion, chopped	2 x 125 g/4 oz cans smoked oysters, drained
3 carrots, chopped	2 tablespoons chopped fresh parsley
300 ml/½ pint water	375 g/12 oz puff pastry, thawed if frozen
½ teaspoon dried thyme	salt and pepper
1 tablespoon soy sauce	beaten egg, to glaze

1 Combine the steak, onion and carrots in a large saucepan. Add the water, thyme and soy sauce with salt and pepper to taste. Bring to the boil, then lower the heat, cover and simmer for about 1½ hours, until the meat is tender.

2 Taste and add more seasoning if necessary. In a cup, blend the cornflour to a paste with a little water. Stir into the pan, and simmer until the sauce is thickened and smooth. Stir in the oysters and parsley and leave to cool.

3 Roll out half of the pastry on a lightly floured surface and line a 1.2 litre/2 pint oven-proof dish or a 23 cm/9 inch pie plate. Place the cooled meat mixture over the pastry. Dampen the edges with water. Roll out the remaining pastry and cover the pie. Trim the edges, then knock back the edges with a knife and flute to seal and decorate.

4 Reroll the pastry trimmings and cut into stars or leaves. Attach to the pie with a little of the beaten egg. Brush the top of the pie with beaten egg and bake in a preheated oven, 220°C (425°F), Gas Mark 7, for 35–40 minutes, until the pastry is crisp and golden brown. Serve hot with mashed potatoes, and a green vegetable such as cabbage or Brussels sprouts.

Serves 6
Preparation time:
Cooking time: 35–40 minutes
Oven temperature: 220°C (425°F), Gas Mark 7

Bean Sprout Salad

This crunchy, fresh-tasting salad is very refreshing after all the heavy Christmas meals. It is very easy to prepare, and is ideal for vegetarians.

- 125 g/4 oz button mushrooms, thinly sliced
- 2 tablespoons French dressing
- 500 g/1 lb fresh bean sprouts or 2 x 410 g/13½ oz cans bean sprouts, well drained
- 4 carrots, trimmed and cut into thin sticks
- 250 g/8 oz red cabbage, thinly shredded
- 3 cartons mustard and cress

1 Put the mushrooms into a large salad bowl and pour over the French dressing. Toss lightly and leave to stand for 30 minutes.
2 Add all the remaining ingredients and toss well. Serve at once.

Serves 4
Preparation time: 20 minutes, plus standing

Bean and Mushroom Salad

- 1 x 440 g/15½ oz can butter beans, drained
- 1 x 440 g/15½ oz can red kidney beans, drained
- 1 x 400 g/13 oz can flageolet beans, drained
- 1 x 375 g/12 oz can sweetcorn kernels, drained
- 125 g/4 oz button mushrooms, quartered
- 1 bunch spring onions, finely chopped

DRESSING:

- 4 tablespoons olive oil
- 1–2 tablespoons wine vinegar
- ¼ teaspoon mustard powder
- 1 garlic clove, finely chopped
- salt and pepper

1 In a large salad bowl, mix together the butter beans, red kidney and flageolet beans, sweetcorn, mushrooms and spring onions, reserving a tablespoon of spring onions for the garnish.
2 Put all the dressing ingredients into a screw-top jar and shake vigorously. Pour over the salad and toss well. Sprinkle the reserved spring onions over the top, to garnish.

Serves 8–10
Preparation time: 10–15 minutes

Chicken Galantine

A boned chicken makes a wonderful natural casing for a stuffing, and is neat and easy to carve. Galantines, served sliced, cold, are ideal for buffets and large parties.

- 2 kg/4 lb chicken
- 250 g/8 oz sausagemeat
- 250 g/8 oz minced veal
- 1 onion, finely chopped
- 1 tablespoon green peppercorns, drained
- grated rind and juice of ½ lemon
- 2 tablespoons dry sherry
- 50 g/2 oz pressed tongue, sliced
- 50 g/2 oz mushrooms, finely chopped
- 4 tablespoons finely chopped fresh parsley
- 25 g/1 oz fresh white breadcrumbs
- 1 tablespoon capers, drained and chopped
- 25 g/1 oz butter, melted
- 1 tablespoon oil
- salt and pepper
- holly sprigs, to decorate

1 To bone the chicken, set it on a board breast side down. Cut through the skin along the backbone from the neck to the tail. Be careful not to cut the skin from now on. Scrape the flesh away from the bones, gradually working around the carcass, breaking the legs and wings away from the rib cage as you go. Cut off the ends of the wing and leg joints, and pull out the rib cage. Remove the breastbone gently, being very careful not to tear the skin along the breastbone. Using a small knife, scrape the flesh from the leg and wing bones.

2 Spread out the boned bird on a work surface, skin side down. Fold the legs and wings towards the inside. Trim the bird to a neat rectangular shape. Spread a sheet of greaseproof paper over the flesh and beat with a rolling pin to flatten.

3 Mix together the sausagemeat and minced veal in a large bowl. Stir in the onion, peppercorns, lemon rind and juice and sherry. Season with pepper.

4 Spread the mixture over the inside of the chicken and lay the tongue on top. Mix together the mushrooms, parsley, breadcrumbs and capers. Season and lay the mixture over the tongue. Bring up the sides of the skin to enclose the filling and fasten along the top with a skewer. Bring up the ends and sew with a needle and thread to make a neat rectangular shape. Weigh the roll.

5 Place the roll on a large sheet of foil in a roasting tin. Brush all over with butter and oil, then seal the foil. Bake in a preheated oven, 180°C (350°F), Gas Mark 4, for 30 minutes per 500g/1 lb.

6 Open the foil, baste and cook for a final 30 minutes until golden brown. To test if the galantine is cooked, insert a skewer; the juices should run clear. Remove from the foil and place on a wire rack to cool. Remove the threads. Slice thinly and decorate with holly sprigs to serve.

Serves 8–10
Preparation time: 1 hour
Cooking time: about 2½–2¾ hours
Oven temperature: 180°C (350°F), Gas Mark 4

Parsnip Duchesse Potatoes

- 750 g/1½ lb parsnips, peeled and cut into equal-sized pieces
- 750 g/1½ lb potatoes, peeled and cut into chunks
- pinch of ground nutmeg
- 1 egg
- salt and pepper

1 Cook the parsnips and potatoes in separate pans of salted boiling water for about 20 minutes, until tender.

2 Drain well, then mash together. Beat until smooth, then rub through a sieve. Turn the mixture into a bowl, season well with salt and pepper and beat in the nutmeg and egg.

3 Spoon the vegetable mixture into a piping bag fitted with a large star nozzle and pipe large whirls of the mixture on to a greased baking sheet.

4 Bake in a preheated oven, 200°C (400°F), Gas Mark 6, for about 25 minutes until lightly browned. Serve hot.

Serves 6
Preparation time: 20 minutes
Cooking time: about 50 minutes
Oven temperature: 200°C (400°F), Gas Mark 6

Blackcurrant Sorbet

- 500 g/1 lb blackcurrants
- 150 ml/¼ pint water
- 125 g/4 oz caster sugar
- 2 tablespoons lemon juice
- 1 egg white, lightly whisked
- mint leaves, to garnish

1 Place the blackcurrants in a saucepan with 2 tablespoons of the water and simmer until tender. Rub through a sieve: there should be 300 ml/ ½ pint blackcurrant purée.
2 Place the sugar and the remaining water in a saucepan and heat gently, stirring constantly, until dissolved. Bring to the boil and simmer for 5 minutes. Leave to cool.
3 Add the sugar syrup to the blackcurrant purée with the lemon juice. Turn the purée into a rigid freezerproof container. Cover and freeze until partially set.
4 When the sorbet is half frozen, fold in the egg white. Freeze until firm. Transfer the sorbet to the refrigerator 10 minutes before serving to soften a little. Serve on chilled plates.

Serves 4
Preparation time: 15 minutes, plus freezing
Cooking time: 15 minutes

Leftover
Turkey Ideas

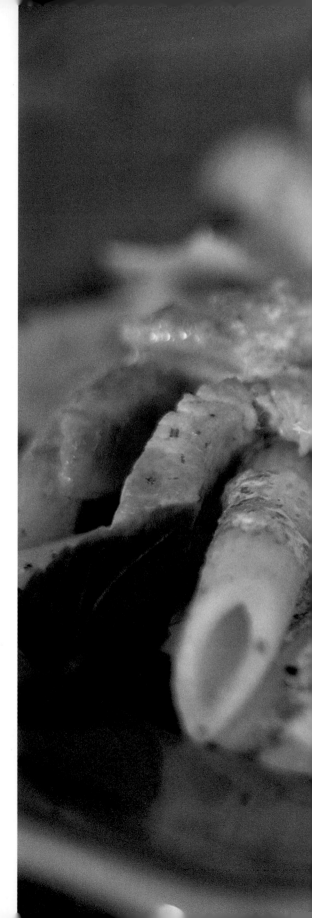

Penne with Turkey and Pesto

2 tablespoons extra-virgin olive oil

250 g/8 oz penne or other dried pasta shapes

375 g/12 oz cooked turkey, cut diagonally into thin strips

3 tablespoons ready-made pesto

4–6 tablespoons double cream

salt and pepper

TO GARNISH:

shavings of Parmesan cheese

basil leaves

1 Add 1 tablespoon of the oil and ½ teaspoon salt to a large saucepan of boiling water. Add the penne or other pasta shapes. Boil, uncovered, for about 10 minutes, or according to the packet instructions, until *al dente*.

2 Meanwhile, heat a wok or large deep frying pan over a moderate heat until hot, add the remaining oil and heat until hot but not smoking. Add the turkey and stir-fry for 1–2 minutes.

3 Add the pesto and stir-fry for 2–3 minutes until the turkey is heated through.

4 Drain the pasta well, add to the turkey mixture and toss over a high heat until evenly mixed with the turkey and pesto. Add the cream, and salt and pepper to taste, and toss well to mix. Serve in warmed bowls or soup plates and garnish with shavings of Parmesan and basil leaves.

Serves 3–4

Preparation time: 5 minutes

Cooking time: 10–15 minutes

Warm Salad of Turkey, Red Pepper and Lemon

- 2 Little Gem lettuces, leaves separated
- 1 red pepper, cored, deseeded and cut lengthways into thin strips
- 2 tablespoons extra-virgin olive oil
- 500 g/1 lb cooked turkey, cut diagonally into thin strips
- lemon wedges, to garnish

DRESSING:

- 3 tablespoons extra-virgin olive oil
- 2 tablespoons lemon juice
- 1 garlic clove, crushed
- 1 teaspoon Dijon mustard
- salt and pepper

1 Whisk the dressing ingredients in a bowl until thickened. Tear the lettuce leaves roughly and put them into a large salad bowl.

2 Fry the red pepper strips in the oil, stirring frequently, for 5 minutes. Add the turkey strips and cook, stirring, for another 5 minutes until tender and cooked through.

3 Remove the turkey and pepper strips from the pan with a slotted spoon and arrange on top of the lettuce.

4 Pour the dressing into the pan, increase the heat to high and stir until sizzling. Pour the dressing over the salad and toss. Serve at once, garnished with lemon wedges.

Serves 4
Preparation time: 10 minutes
Cooking time: 10 minutes

Turkey au Gratin

- 500 g/1 lb cooked turkey, chopped
- 25 g/1 oz butter
- 125 g/4 oz blanched almonds
- 50 g/2 oz Parmesan cheese, grated
- 4 tablespoons chopped fresh parsley
- 75 g/3 oz brown breadcrumbs

SAUCE:

- 25 g/1 oz butter or margarine
- 25 g/1 oz plain flour
- 600 ml/1 pint milk
- 50 g/2 oz Cheddar cheese, grated
- 1 garlic clove, crushed
- salt and pepper

1 Arrange the turkey in a shallow ovenproof dish. Melt the butter in a saucepan, add the almonds and toss until golden. Sprinkle the nuts and butter over the turkey.

2 To make the sauce, melt the butter in a saucepan. Sprinkle in the flour and cook, stirring, for 1–2 minutes. Add the milk, a little at a time, stirring after each addition, then simmer for 2 minutes. Add the grated Cheddar cheese and garlic, season to taste, and stir until the cheese has melted.

3 Pour the sauce over the turkey. Mix together the Parmesan, parsley and breadcrumbs and sprinkle evenly over the turkey. Bake in a preheated oven, 160°C (325°F), Gas Mark 3, for 30–40 minutes until golden.

Serves 4

Preparation time: 15 minutes
Cooking time: 30–40 minutes
Oven temperature: 160°C (325°F), Gas Mark 3

Country Turkey Pie

- 50 g/2 oz butter
- 40 g/1½ oz plain flour
- 750 ml/1¼ pints milk
- 1½ chicken stock cubes, crumbled
- ½ teaspoon Worcestershire sauce
- 1½ tablespoons dry sherry
- 3 drops of Tabasco sauce
- 375 g/12 oz cooked turkey, diced
- 175 g/6 oz mushrooms, sliced
- 250 g/8 oz carrots, cooked and sliced
- 250 g/8 oz button onions, boiled
- 300 g/10 oz packet puff pastry
- beaten egg, to glaze
- freshly grated Parmesan cheese
- salt

1 Melt the butter in a large saucepan, sprinkle in the flour and cook for 1 minute. Add the milk, a little at a time, stirring after each addition, then add the stock cubes and Worcestershire sauce and season with salt. Bring to the boil, stirring with a wooden spoon until the mixture thickens. Stir in the sherry and Tabasco sauce. Add the turkey, mushrooms, carrots and onions and heat through gently but thoroughly. Turn the mixture into a 1.8 litre/3 pint pie dish.
2 Roll out the pastry on a lightly floured surface and cover the dish, fluting the edges of the pastry against the rim. Make a small hole in the centre of the pastry in order to allow the steam to escape. Decorate with the pastry trimmings – stars or holly leaves would be seasonal. Bake the pie in a preheated oven, 200°C (400°F), Gas Mark 6, for about 20 minutes until the pastry begins to brown.
3 Brush the top of the pie with beaten egg and sprinkle with the Parmesan. Return to the oven for a further 10 minutes until the pastry is puffed up and brown.

Serves 6
Preparation time: 20 minutes
Cooking time: about 30 minutes
Oven temperature: 200°C (400°F), Gas Mark 6

VARIATION

Turkey, Ham and Almond Pie

- 40 g/1½ oz butter
- 25 g/1 oz almonds
- 25 g/1 oz plain flour
- 150 ml/¼ pint dry white wine
- 300 ml/½ pint chicken stock
- ½ teaspoon dried marjoram
- 2 tablespoons soured cream
- 125 g/4 oz green or black grapes, halved and seeded
- 375 g/12 oz cooked turkey, diced
- 125 g/4 oz bacon or ham, diced
- salt and pepper

1 Melt the butter in a frying pan, add the almonds and fry over moderate heat until browned. Stir in the flour, remove from the heat and stir until blended. Gradually stir in the wine and stock and bring to the boil, then lower the heat and simmer for 1–2 minutes.
2 Season well, add the marjoram and stir in the cream. Turn into a large bowl. Mix in the grapes, turkey and ham, then turn the filling into a 1.8 litre/3 pint pie dish.
3 Cover and bake the pie as in the main recipe.

Turkey Crumble

- 2 carrots, trimmed and thinly sliced
- 1 leek, sliced
- 40 g/1½ oz butter
- 1 onion, finely chopped
- 40 g/1½ oz plain flour
- 250 ml/8 fl oz turkey or chicken stock
- 1 x 375 g/12 oz can sweetcorn with peppers, drained and juice reserved
- 250 g/8 oz cooked turkey, cut into chunks
- salt and pepper

TOPPING:
- 75 g/3 oz wholemeal flour
- 50 g/2 oz chilled butter
- 75 g/3 oz wholemeal breadcrumbs
- 25 g/1 oz grated cheese
- 1 tablespoon chopped fresh parsley

1 Boil the carrots in lightly salted water for 10 minutes. Add the leek and cook for a further 5–8 minutes. The vegetables should retain a slight 'bite'. Drain and refresh under cold water. Drain again and set aside.

2 Melt the butter in a large saucepan over a moderate heat. Add the onion and cook until softened but not browned. Add the flour and cook, stirring, for 2 minutes. Remove from the heat and gradually stir in the stock and reserved can juices. Return to the heat and cook, stirring constantly, until the sauce has thickened and is almost boiling. Season to taste with salt and pepper. Add the cooked turkey and mix well. Transfer the mixture to a buttered ovenproof dish and set aside.

3 To make the topping, place the flour in a bowl. Add the butter and rub in lightly with the fingertips until the mixture resembles fine breadcrumbs. Season lightly and stir in the breadcrumbs, cheese and parsley. Spoon the topping over the turkey and vegetable mixture and bake in the centre of a preheated oven, 190°C (375°F), Gas Mark 5, for 35–40 minutes or until the topping is crisp and golden brown.

Serves 6
Preparation time: 35 minutes
Cooking time: about 35–40 minutes
Oven temperature: 190°C (375°F), Gas Mark 5

Stir-fried Turkey with Pine Nuts and Green Peppers

- 3 tablespoons rapeseed oil
- 50 g/2 oz pine nuts
- 1 onion, thinly sliced
- 2.5 cm/1 inch piece of fresh root ginger, peeled and very thinly sliced
- 2 green peppers, cored, deseeded and cut lengthways into thin strips
- 500 g/1 lb cooked turkey, cut diagonally into thin strips
- salt and pepper

SAUCE:
- 2 teaspoons cornflour
- 2 tablespoons water
- 2 tablespoons soy sauce
- 2 tablespoons rice wine or dry sherry
- 1 tablespoon wine vinegar
- 1 garlic clove, crushed
- 1 teaspoon soft dark brown sugar

1 To make the sauce, blend the cornflour and water, add the remaining sauce ingredients and set aside.

2 Heat 1 tablespoon of the oil in a wok, add the pine nuts and toss for 1–2 minutes until golden brown. Remove and drain on kitchen paper.

3 Gently stir-fry the onion, ginger and green peppers in the remaining oil for 3–4 minutes until softened but not coloured. Remove and set aside.

4 Stir-fry the turkey for 1–2 minutes until heated through.

5 Whisk the sauce, add to the wok and bring to the boil, stirring until it has thickened. Add the pepper mixture and toss to mix, then add the pine nuts and toss again. Season to taste and serve with Chinese noodles.

Serves 4
Preparation time: 15 minutes
Cooking time: 10–15 minutes

Christmas
Nibbles

Crispy Ricotta Parcels

250 g/8 oz ricotta cheese

125 g/4 oz frozen spinach, thawed, chopped and squeezed dry

125 g/4 oz smoked ham, finely chopped

¼ teaspoon ground nutmeg

8 sheets filo pastry

75 g/3 oz butter, melted

pepper

1 Place the ricotta cheese in a bowl with the spinach, ham and nutmeg and add pepper to taste. Mix well.

2 Put the sheets of filo pastry on a plate and cover with a damp tea towel. Working with one sheet of pastry at a time, cut it into three equal strips and brush well with butter. Place a teaspoon of the cheese mixture at one end of each strip. Fold the pastry diagonally over to enclose the filling in a triangle of pastry and continue folding to make a neat triangular parcel.

3 Brush the parcel with more butter and place on a baking sheet. Repeat with the remaining filling, pastry and butter, to make 24 small parcels.

4 Bake the parcels in a preheated oven, 220°C (425°F), Gas Mark 7, for 8–10 minutes until golden brown. Serve hot.

Makes 24

Preparation time: 30 minutes

Cooking time: 8–10 minutes

Oven temperature: 220°C (425°F), Gas Mark 7

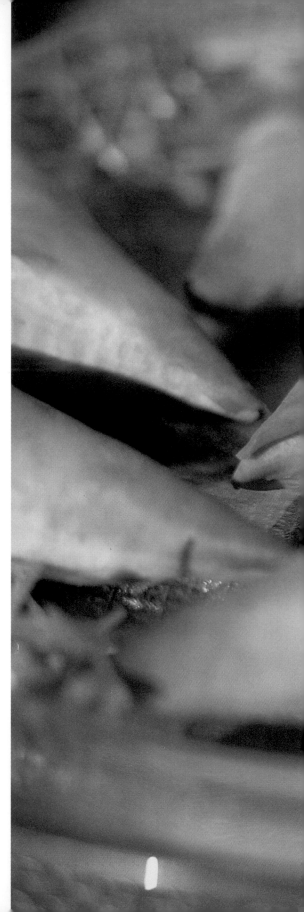

Quick Curried Nuts

These deliciously spicy nuts are wonderful served almost straight from the oven, whilst still warm.

- 40 g/1½ oz butter or sunflower oil
- 1 tablespoon curry powder with whole spices
- 500 g/1 lb mixed skinned nuts, such as almonds, brazils, walnuts, pecans and hazelnuts
- 1 teaspoon salt

1 Melt the butter in a roasting tin and stir in the curry powder. Cook, stirring, for 30 seconds. Add the nuts and stir until well coated.
2 Roast in the oven at 150°C (300°F), Gas Mark 2 for 30 minutes, stirring from time to time.
3 Remove from the oven and toss the nuts with the salt. Allow to cool completely and store in an airtight container for up to 2 weeks.

Makes: 500 g/1 lb
Preparation time: 2 minutes, plus cooling
Cooking time: 32 minutes
Oven temperature: 150°C (300°F), Gas Mark 2

Seasonal Nuts

- **6 tablespoons corn oil**
- **75 g/3 oz butter**
- **500 g/1 lb shelled mixed nuts, such as almonds, peanuts, cashews and walnuts, mixed**
- **salt**

1 Heat the oil and butter in a frying pan until foaming. Add the nuts and fry for 5 minutes, shaking the pan, until browned all over. Remove from the pan with a slotted spoon and drain well on kitchen paper.

2 To serve, sprinkle the nuts with salt to taste, leave to cool, then heap into serving dishes or bowls.

Makes 500 g/1 lb
Preparation time: 2 minutes, plus cooling
Cooking time: 6 minutes

Chicken Liver and Bacon Kebabs

- 375g/12 oz chicken livers
- 375g/12 oz rashers of streaky bacon, rinded
- 4 teaspoons Worcestershire sauce
- 4 teaspoon mushroom ketchup
- 2 tablespoons mustard powder
- 1 teaspoon lemon juice
- 1 tablespoon tomato purée
- 50 g/2 oz butter, melted
- radicchio and rocket leaves, to serve
- lemon wedges, to garnish

1 Trim the chicken livers and cut into 2.5cm/1 inch pieces. Stretch the bacon rashers with the back of a knife. Cut each rasher into two and roll up the pieces with the point of a knife.

2 Thread the liver pieces and bacon rolls alternately on to small skewers. Blend together the Worcestershire sauce, mushroom ketchup, mustard, lemon juice, tomato purée and butter. Place the kebabs close together in a deep dish and pour the sauce over them. Cover closely and marinate in the refrigerator overnight.

3 Place the kebabs on a grill rack and cook under a preheated hot grill for 5–10 minutes, turning and basting with the sauce as they cook. Serve hot with the radicchio and rocket leaves and garnish with lemon wedges.

Serves 8
Preparation time: 10 minutes, plus marinating
Cooking time: 5–10 minutes

VARIATION

Mussel and Bacon Kebabs

Use 2.4 litres/4 pints of fresh mussels or 375 g/12 oz frozen ones, defrosted, instead of the chicken livers. Steam the fresh mussels in a little water for 10 minutes until they open. Discard any mussels that fail to open. Remove the mussels from their shells and thread on to the skewers with the bacon rolls. Blend the marinade, substituting 2 crushed garlic cloves for the mustard. Marinate for 2 hours, then grill as in the main recipe.

Pork and Port Pâté

- 1 large onion
- 1 garlic clove
- 500 g/1 lb belly pork
- small glass of port
- 1 teaspoon fresh mint, chopped
- 250 g/8 oz lambs' liver, finely chopped
- 3 rashers of streaky bacon, finely chopped
- 50 g/2 oz mushrooms, finely chopped
- 1 egg, beaten
- salt and pepper
- rosemary sprigs, to garnish

1 Put the onion, garlic and pork into a food processor and work until smooth. Turn into a bowl, stir in the port and mint and season to taste. Cover closely and leave to marinate in the refrigerator overnight.

2 Mix the lambs' liver, bacon and mushrooms into the pork mixture. Stir in the egg. Spoon into a foil-lined 500 g/1lb loaf tin and bake in a pre-heated oven, 180°C (350°F), Gas Mark 4, for 1½ hours. Carefully pour off the fat and leave to cool.

3 To serve, remove the pâté from the tin, place on a serving dish and garnish with sprigs of rosemary.

Serves 8
Preparation time: 10–15 minutes, plus marinating and cooling
Cooking time: 1½ hours
Oven temperature: 180°C (350°F), Gas Mark 4

Smoked Salmon Blinis

- 250–300 ml/8–10 fl oz milk
- 10 g/⅓ oz fresh yeast or 15 g/½ oz fast-action dried yeast
- 4 tablespoons water
- 50 g/2 oz plain flour
- 100 g/3½ oz buckwheat flour
- ½ teaspoon salt
- 50 g/2 oz butter
- 2 eggs, separated
- 2 tablespoons soured cream

TO SERVE:
- 125 g/4 oz smoked salmon
- 175 g/6 oz crème fraîche

TO GARNISH:
- salmon eggs
- dill sprigs

1 Pour 175 ml/6 fl oz of the milk into a pan. Heat until the milk rises, remove from the heat and allow it to cool.
2 If using fresh yeast, mix with the water. Leave for 5 minutes until frothy. Sift the flours and salt into a bowl. Mix thoroughly, then make a well in the centre. Add the yeast and the scalded milk, and gradually incorporate the flour. Beat for 2 minutes until smooth. Cover with a damp tea towel and put in a warm place for 2–3 hours to rise.
3 Melt half of the butter in a pan and allow to cool a little. Add a further 50 ml/2 fl oz of the milk to the risen batter, stir it in thoroughly. Stir in the egg yolks, soured cream and melted butter until the mixture has the consistency of double cream. (If it is too thick to pour, add more milk.)

4 Whisk the egg whites until stiff peaks form. Fold into the batter, a little at a time, until thoroughly mixed.
5 Heat half of the remaining butter in a frying pan. Pour enough batter into the pan to make a small pancake. Cook for 1–2 minutes, turning when browned. Keep warm while making the remaining blinis. Add more butter

to the pan as necessary until all the batter is used. Serve hot with smoked salmon and crème fraîche, and garnished with salmon eggs and dill sprigs.

Makes 8
Preparation time: 10 minutes, plus standing

Houmous

- 250 g/8 oz chick peas, soaked overnight and drained
- 2–3 garlic cloves
- 250 ml/8 fl oz lemon juice
- 5 tablespoons tahini
- salt
- olive oil
- Kalamata olives, to garnish
- cheese straws, to serve

1 Place the chick peas in a large saucepan of boiling water and cook for 1–1½ hours until soft. Drain and reserve the cooking liquid. Purée the chick peas in a liquidizer or food processor with a little of the cooking liquid, then press the purée through a sieve to remove the skins.

2 Crush the garlic with a little salt and beat into the chick pea purée. Stir in alternate spoonfuls of the lemon juice and tahini, tasting as you go to adjust the flavour. Add more of the cooking liquid if needed, to make a soft, creamy consistency. Taste and adjust the seasoning if necessary. Spoon into a shallow serving dish and chill in the refrigerator for several hours.

3 Remove the houmous from the refrigerator about 10 minutes before serving. Create swirls on the surface with the back of a spoon, then drizzle with olive oil and garnish with olives. Serve with cheese straws.

Serves 6
Preparation time: 10–15 minutes, plus chilling
Cooking time: 1–1½ hours

Taramasalata

- 75 g/3 oz fresh white bread
- 2 tablespoons milk
- 125 g/4 oz smoked cod's roe, skinned
- 1 large garlic clove, crushed
- 125 ml/4 fl oz olive oil
- 2 tablespoons lemon juice
- Kalamata olives, to garnish
- pitta bread, to serve

1 Trim the crusts from the bread and soak the bread slices in the milk for about 15 minutes. Remove the bread slices and squeeze them as dry as possible. Mash the bread with the smoked cod's roe and crushed garlic.

2 Put the mixture into a liquidizer or food processor and gradually add the olive oil, a little at a time, blending well after each addition. Add the lemon juice and blend until smooth. Turn the taramasalata into a bowl, cover and chill in the refrigerator for at least 1 hour.

3 Garnish with olives and serve with warm pitta bread.

Serves 4
Preparation time: 25 minutes, plus chilling

Guacamole

Cover the guacamole tightly with clingfilm until ready to serve.

- 2 large ripe avocados
- 3 tablespoons lemon or lime juice
- 2 garlic cloves, crushed
- 40 g/1½ oz chopped spring onions
- 1–2 tablespoons chopped mild green chillies
- 2 tablespoons chopped fresh coriander
- 125 g/4 oz skinned, seeded and chopped tomatoes
- salt and pepper

TORTILLA CHIPS:

- 8 corn or wheat tortillas
- oil, for deep-frying
- sea salt

1 Cut the avocados in half and remove the stones. Scoop out the flesh and sprinkle with a little of the lemon or lime juice to prevent it discolouring.
2 Put the avocado flesh into a bowl with the remaining lemon juice and mash coarsely. Add the garlic, spring onions, chillies and coriander, and season to taste. Mix in the chopped tomatoes. Cover closely and chill in the refrigerator for at least 1 hour.
3 Meanwhile, make the tortilla chips. Cut each tortilla into 8 equal-sized pieces. Heat the oil in a deep-fat fryer to 180–190°C (350–375°F) or until a cube of bread browns in 30 seconds. Add the tortilla chips and deep-fry until crisp and golden. Drain on kitchen paper and sprinkle with a little sea salt. Serve with the guacamole.

Serves 6
Preparation time: 15 minutes, plus chilling
Cooking time: 5 minutes

Christmas Drinks

White Wine Punch

3 bottles dry white wine, well chilled

½–¾ bottle dry sherry

4–6 tablespoons Curaçao or Grand Marnier

900 ml/1½ pints tonic water, well chilled, or 450 ml/¾ pint each tonic water and

lemonade, well chilled

crushed ice

TO DECORATE:

cucumber slices

1 orange, thinly sliced

1 lemon, thinly sliced

1 apple, cored and sliced

1 Pour the white wine, sherry, Curaçao or Grand Marnier into a large bowl. Cover and chill in the refrigerator until required.

2 Just before serving, add the tonic water or tonic water and lemonade mixture.

3 To serve, put a handful of crushed ice into the bottom of serving jugs and add the punch. Decorate the jugs of punch with the cucumber, orange, lemon and apple slices.

Serves 20

Preparation time: 15 minutes

Claret Cup

- 75 ml/3 fl oz white rum
- 1 miniature bottle of orange-flavoured liqueur
- thinly peeled rind of 1 lemon
- 2 bottles claret or other red wine
- 3 bottles ginger ale
- ice cubes

1 Put the rum and orange-flavoured liqueur into a small jug. Add the lemon rind, cover and leave to marinate for about 2 hours.
2 Pour the claret and ginger ale into a large bowl, add the rum and orange-flavoured liqueur mixture with the lemon rind and stir to mix. Add a handful of ice cubes and serve at once.

Serves 12
Preparation time: 10 minutes, plus marinating

Heartwarmer

- 200 ml/7 fl oz red grape juice
- 250 g/8 oz brown sugar
- 350 ml/12 fl oz dark rum
- 1.5 litres/2½ pints dry white wine
- 450 ml/¾ pint red wine

1 Put the grape juice into a saucepan, add the sugar and stir over a gentle heat until the sugar has completely dissolved. Stir in the dark rum and set aside.

2 Pour the white wine and red wine into a large saucepan and heat until hot but not boiling. Add the rum and grape juice mixture and stir together. Serve hot.

Serves 12
Cooking time: 10 minutes

Spiced Mulled Wine

This spiced mulled wine is ideal after a cold Christmas walk or to welcome guests on a winter evening.

- **1 bottle red wine**
- **¼ bottle inexpensive port**
- **600 ml/1 pint boiling water**
- **brown or white sugar, to taste**
- **pinch of ground nutmeg**
- **1 cinnamon stick**
- **pared orange rind**

1 Heat the red wine and port in a saucepan until almost boiling. Add the boiling water. Stir in the sugar and nutmeg, pour into a large bowl and add a cinnamon stick and some pared orange rind.

Serves 10
Cooking time: 5 minutes

Mulled Ale

Mulls were traditionally mixed at the fireside and heated by plunging a red-hot poker into the pan.

- **1.2 litres/2 pints brown ale**
- **150 ml/¼ pint rum or brandy**
- **3 tablespoons brown sugar**
- **6 cloves**
- **1 teaspoon ground ginger**
- **pinch of ground nutmeg**
- **pinch of ground cinnamon**
- **thinly peeled rind and juice of 1 lemon**
- **thinly peeled rind and juice of 1 orange**
- **600 ml/1 pint water**
- **orange slice, to decorate (optional)**

1 Put all the ingredients into a large saucepan. Bring slowly to the boil, stirring all the time to dissolve the sugar. Turn off the heat and leave to stand for a few minutes.
2 To serve, strain into a warmed jug and float an orange slice on top, if you like.

Serves 12
Cooking time: 10 minutes, plus standing

Loving Cup

An ideal drink to welcome guests on Christmas day.

- **8 sugar cubes**
- **2 lemons**
- **½ bottle medium-sweet or sweet sherry**
- **¼ bottle brandy**
- **1 bottle dry sparkling white wine**

1 Rub the sugar cubes over the lemons to absorb the zest. Thinly peel the lemons and remove as much of the pith as possible. Thinly slice the lemons and set aside.

2 Put the lemon rind, sherry, brandy and sugar cubes into a jug and stir until the sugar is dissolved. Cover and chill in the refrigerator for about 30 minutes.

3 To serve, add the wine to the cup and float the lemon slices on top.

Serves 12
Preparation time: 10 minutes, plus chilling

Champagne Strawberry Cup

- 175 ml/6 fl oz fraises des bois or other strawberry liqueur, chilled
- 1 bottle non-vintage dry champagne or dry sparkling white wine, chilled
- 125 g/4 oz strawberries, sliced

1 Pour the fraises des bois into a large jug. Gradually add the champagne or dry sparkling wine, stirring very gently so as not to lose the bubbles.
2 Divide the strawberry slices among individual glasses and top up with strawberry-flavoured champagne. Serve at once.

Serves 6
Preparation time: 5 minutes

Brandy and Lemon Sparkler

- juice of 15 lemons
- juice of 4 oranges
- 625 g/1¼ lb caster sugar
- ice cubes (optional)
- 300 ml/½ pint orange Curaçao
- 2 measures grenadine
- 2.4 litres/4 pints brandy
- 2.4 litres/4 pints sparkling mineral water

TO DECORATE:
- lemon slices
- orange slices

1 Pour the lemon and orange juices into a jug. Add the caster sugar and stir until dissolved.
2 To serve, put the ice cubes, if using, into a punch bowl. Add the lemon and orange juice mixture and the remaining ingredients. Stir well. Decorate with the lemon and orange slices.

Serves 30
Preparation time: 10–15 minutes

Fruit Punch

A delicious non-alcoholic punch, ideal for children.

- **600 ml/1 pint orange juice**
- **600 ml/1 pint apple juice**
- **150 ml/¼ pint water**
- **½ teaspoon ground ginger**
- **½ teaspoon mixed spice**
- **brown or white sugar (optional)**
- **1 apple, thinly sliced, to decorate**

1 Place the orange and apple juices, water and spices in a saucepan and bring gently to the boil, adding sugar to taste if required. Simmer the mixture for 5 minutes.

2 Pour the punch into a warmed bowl and float the apple slices on top.

Serves 6
Preparation time: 5 minutes
Cooking time: 10 minutes

Grape Punch

An unusual non-alcoholic punch.

- **600 ml/1 pint sparkling apple juice**
- **600 ml/1 pint grape juice**
- **600 ml/1 pint ginger ale**
- **4 tablespoons lime juice cordial**
- **4 tablespoons clear honey**

TEA LIQUOR:
- **25 g/1 oz Indian tea leaves**
- **600 ml/1 pint cold water**

TO DECORATE:
- **ice cubes (optional)**
- **12 lemon slices**
- **seedless grapes**

1 First make the tea liquor. Put the Indian tea leaves into a jug and pour over the cold water. Cover and leave to stand overnight.
2 Measure 450 ml/¾ pint of the tea liquor into a large bowl, add the remaining ingredients and stir well.
3 To serve, pour the punch into individual glasses, add the ice cubes, if liked, and decorate with the speared lemon slices and seedless grapes.

Serves 12
Preparation time: 10 minutes, plus standing

Cranberry Crush

- crushed ice
- 1.8 litres/3 pints sweetened cranberry juice
- 600 ml/1 pint fresh orange juice
- 600 ml/1 pint ginger ale
- orange and lemon wedges, to decorate

1 Half fill a large punch bowl with crushed ice. Pour in the cranberry juice and orange juice and stir to mix.
2 Top up with the ginger ale and decorate with orange and lemon wedges. Serve at once.

Serves 15
Preparation time: 5 minutes

Recipe Photographer: Sandra Lane
Recipe Home Economist: Maxine Clark
Jacket Photographer: Gus Filgate
Jacket Home Economist: Louise Pickford